COLLINS GEM

Portuguese
PHRASE FINDER

HarperCollins*Publishers*

CONSULTANT
Edite Vieira

OTHER GEM PHRASE FINDERS

DUTCH
FRENCH
GERMAN
GREEK
ITALIAN
SLOVENE
SPANISH
TURKISH

Look out for Phrase Finder Tape Packs!

First published 1995

Reprint 10 9 8 7 6 5 4 3 2 1
Printed in Great Britain

ISBN 0 00-470839-3

Your *Collins Gem Phrase Finder* is designed to help you locate the exact phrase you need in any situation, whether for holiday or business. If you want to adapt the phrases, we have made sure that you can easily see where to substitute your own words (you can find them in the dictionary section), and the clear, alphabetical, two-colour layout gives you direct access to the different topics.

The *Phrase Finder* includes:

- Over 70 topics arranged alphabetically from **ACCOMMODATION** to **WORK**. Each phrase is accompanied by a simple pronunciation guide which ensures that there's no problem over pronouncing the foreign words.
- Practical hints and useful vocabulary highlighted in boxes. Where the English words appear first in the box, this indicates vocabulary you may need. Where the red Portuguese words appear first, these are words you are more likely to see written on signs and notices.

WORDS APPEARING IN BLACK ARE ENGLISH WORDS	WORDS APPEARING IN RED ARE PORTUGUESE WORDS

- Possible phrases you may hear in reply to your questions. The foreign phrases appear in red.
- A clearly laid-out 5000-word dictionary: English words appear in black and Portuguese words appear in red.
- A basic grammar section which will enable you to build on your phrases.

It's worth spending time before you embark on your travels just looking through the topics to see what is covered and becoming familiar with what might be said to you.

Whatever the situation, your *Phrase Finder* is sure to help!

BUSINESS

- ACCOUNTS
- BUSINESS–MEETING
- COMPUTERS
- FAX
- IMPORT/EXPORT
- LETTERS
- OFFICE
- WORK

TRAVEL

- *see* CAR
- AIR TRAVEL
- BOAT & FERRY
- BUS
- CUSTOMS CONTROL
- METRO
- TAXI
- TRAIN

EATING & DRINKING

- DRINKING
- EATING OUT
- VEGETARIAN
- WINES & SPIRITS

CAR

- BREAKDOWNS
- CAR–DRIVING
- CAR–HIRE
- CAR–PARTS
- PETROL STATION

DIFFICULTIES

- COMPLAINTS
- EMERGENCIES
- PROBLEMS

LEISURE

- CELEBRATIONS
- CINEMA
- ENTERTAINMENT
- LEISURE/INTERESTS
- MUSIC
- SIGHTSEEING & TOURIST OFFICE
- SPORTS
- TELEVISION
- THEATRE
- WALKING

SHOPPING

- CLOTHES
- FOOD–GENERAL, FRUIT & VEG.
- MAPS, GUIDES & NEWSPAPERS
- PHARMACY
- PHOTOS & VIDEOS
- POST OFFICE
- SHOPPING–SHOPS

ACCOMMODATION

- ACCOMMODATION
- CAMPING
- DISABLED TRAVELLERS
- HOTEL
- PAYING
- ROOM SERVICE
- SIGHTSEEING & TOURIST OFFICE

PRACTICALITIES

- ALPHABET
- BASICS
- COLOUR & SHAPE
- DAYS, MONTHS & SEASONS
- DIRECTIONS
- LAUNDRY
- LUGGAGE
- MEASUREMENTS & QUANTITIES
- MONEY
- NUMBERS
- PAYING
- QUESTIONS
- REPAIRS
- SIGNS & NOTICES
- TELEPHONE
- TIME–TIME PHRASES

MEETING PEOPLE

- BASICS
- CELEBRATIONS
- GREETINGS
- MAKING FRIENDS
- WEATHER
- WORK

HEALTH

- BODY
- DENTIST
- DOCTOR
- EMERGENCIES
- PHARMACY

CONTENTS

LIST OF TOPICS

The Portuguese language is much easier to read than to speak. However, the pronunciation guide used in this book is as near as possible to the real sound. The syllable to be stresssed is marked in ***heavy italics****. Note that in conversation words tend to run together.*

■ VOWELS (a, e, i, o, u)

OPEN (LONG) SOUND	CLOSED (SHORT) SOUND
a *ie.* ***saco*** ***sah****-koo*	*ie.* ***fama*** ***fa****muh*
e *ie.* ***terra*** ***terr****uh*	*ie.* ***de*** *duh*
o *ie.* ***cobra*** ***koh****-bruh*	*ie.* ***voltar*** *vol****tar***

NOTE: *The article* **a** *sounds like uh (as in* **the**), *unless stressed, ie.* **à**
e *can sound like ay, ie.* ***fecho*** ***fay****shoo, but tends to be silent at the end of words, ie.* ***pode*** *pod) unless stressed, ie.* ***bebé***. *The word* **e** *(meaning* **and**) *always sounds like ee (as in* **police**)
o *can sound like oo, ie.* ***vaso*** ***vah****-zoo, and the article* **o** *always sounds like oo*
i *sounds like ee, ie.* ***fica*** ***fee****kuh*
u *usually sounds like oo, ie.* ***luvas*** ***loo****vush*

■ VOWEL COMBINATIONS

ai = *y, ie.* ***mais*** = *mysh* — **oi** = *oy, ie.* ***coisa*** = ***koy****-zuh*
ei = *ay, ie.* ***peixe*** = *paysh* — **ou** = *oh, ie.* ***outro*** = ***oh****-troo*

■ NASAL VOWELS *Vowels with a tilde ~, or followed by m (* **um** *) or n (* **in** *) should be pronounced nasally (let air out through nose as well as mouth), similar to French. We have represented this sound in the pronunciation by ñ, ie.*

tem = *tayñ*	**com** = *koñ*	**um** = *ooñ*
pão = *powñ*	**manhã** = *man-****yañ***	**põe** = *poyñ*

■ OTHER LETTERS *Try to recognize the sounds of the following:*
● **ç** ***serviço*** *ser****vee****soo* ● **nh** ***tenho*** ***ten****-yoo* ● **ch** ***chá*** *sha*
● **r/rr** *at the start or middle of word rolled* ● **g** ***gelo*** ***jay****-loo (soft like zh)* ● **s** *(between vowels)* ***coisa*** ***koy****-zuh; (after vowel and at end of word)* ***está*** *shta,* ***lápis*** ***lah****-peesh* ● **h** *always silent* ● **j** ***loja*** ***lo****juh (soft like zh)* ● **x** ***caixa*** ***ky****-shuh*
● **lh** ***mulher*** *mool-****yehr*** ● **z** *(at end of word)* ***faz*** *fash*

If you haven't booked your accommodation, check with the local tourist office to see if they have a list of hotels and guesthouses.

HOTEL	**HOTEL**	CHEIO	**FULL UP**
QUARTOS	**ROOMS AVAILABLE**	PENSÃO/RESIDENCIAL	**GUESTHOUSE**

Do you have a list of accommodation with prices?
Tem uma lista de hotéis com os preços?
*tayñ **oom**uh **leesh**tuh duh oh-**taysh** koñ oosh **pray**-soosh*

Is there a hotel here?
Há algum hotel aqui?
*a al**gooñ** oh-**tel** a**kee***

Do you have any vacancies?
Tem vagas?
*tayñ **vah**-gush*

I'd like (to book) a room...
Queria (reservar) um quarto...
***kree**-uh (ruh-zer**var**) ooñ **kwar**too...*

with bath
com casa de banho
*koñ **kah**-zuh duh **bahn**-yoo*

single
individual
*eendeeveed-**wal***

double
de casal
*duh ka**zal***

with shower
com chuveiro
*koñ shoo-**vay**roo*

with a double bed
com cama de casal
*koñ **kah**-muh duh ka**zal***

twin-bedded
com duas camas
*koñ **doo**-ush **kah**-mush*

with an extra bed for a child
com uma cama extra para uma criança
*koñ **oom**uh **kah**-muh **aysh**-truh **par**uh **oom**uh kree-**an**suh*

A room that looks...
Um quarto que dê...
*ooñ **kwar**too kuh day...*

onto the garden
para o jardim
*pro jar-**deeñ***

onto the sea
para o mar
*pro **mar***

We'd like two rooms next to each other
Queríamos dois quartos contíguos
***kree**uh-moosh doysh **kwar**toosh kon**teeg**woosh*

CONT...

We'd like to stay ... nights
Queríamos ficar ... noites
kreeuh-moosh feekar ... noytsh

from ... till...
do dia ... ao dia...
doo dee-uh ... ow dee-uh...

I will confirm...
Confirmarei...
komfeer-maray...

by letter
por carta
poor kartuh

by fax
por fax
poor fax

How much is it...?
Qual é o preço...?
kwal e oo pray-soo...

per night
por noite
poor noyt

per week
por semana
poor semah-nuh

for half board
com meia-pensão
koñ may-yuh paynsowñ

full board
com pensão completa
koñ paynsowñ kompletuh

Is breakfast included?
Inclui o pequeno-almoço?
een-klwee oo puh-kaynoo almoh-soo

Have you anything cheaper?
Tem alguma coisa mais barata?
tayñ algoomuh koy-zuh mysh barahtuh

Can you suggest somewhere else?
Pode aconselhar outro sítio?
pod akonsel-yuhr oh-troo seetyoo

■ YOU MAY HEAR

Não temos vagas
nowñ taymoosh vah-gush
We've no vacancies

Estamos cheios
shta-moosh shayoosh
We're full up

Para quantas noites?
paruh kwantush noytsh
For how many nights?

O seu nome, por favor?
oo sayoo nom poor favor
Your name, please?

É favor confirmar...
e favor komfeermar...
Please confirm...

por escrito
poor shkree-too
in writing

por fax
poor fax
by fax

■ CAMPING ■ HOTEL ■ SIGHTSEEING & TOURIST OFFICE

AMOUNT *(of money)*	**A QUANTIA**
DELIVERY NOTE	**A NOTA DE ENTREGA**
DELIVERY TERMS	**AS CONDIÇÕES DE ENTREGA**
ORDER	**A ENCOMENDA**

I'd like to speak to someone in your accounts department
Queria falar com alguém da contabilidade
__kree__-uh fa__lar__ koñ al__gayñ__ duh konta-bee-lee__dahd__

It's regarding invoice number...
É a respeito da factura número...
e uh rush-__pay__too duh fak__too__ruh __noo__meroo...

I think there is an error
Creio que há um erro
__kray__oo kuh a ooñ __err__oo

We are still waiting for the invoice to be settled
Estamos ainda à espera que a factura seja liquidada
__shtuh__-mooz a-__een__duh a __shpeh__ruh kuh uh fak__too__ruh __say__-juh lee-__kee__daduh

Please supply a credit note and new invoice
Por favor envie uma nota de crédito e nova factura
poor fa__vor__ en-__vee__-uh __oom__uh __no__ta duh __kred__itoo ee __noh__-vuh fak__too__ruh

Please address the invoice to...
Por favor passe a factura em nome de...
poor fa__vor__ __pa__ss uh fak__too__ruh ayñ nom duh...

The goods should be accompanied by a pro forma invoice
As mercadorias devem ser acompanhadas por uma factura pro-forma *ush merka-doo__ree__ush __dev__ayñ ser akompan-__yah__-dush poor __oom__uh fak__too__ruh pro__for__ma*

Please state content and value of the consignment
Por favor especifique o conteúdo e valor do envio
poor fa__vor__ shpuhsee-__feek__ oo kont__yoo__-doo ee va__lor__ doo en__vee__-oo

■ NUMBERS ■ TELEPHONE

Most signs are in Portuguese and English and you may go through the airport without having to speak any Portuguese. Here are a few signs you will find useful to know. The blue customs channel is for EC citizens travelling within Europe who have no goods to declare.

CHEGADAS	**ARRIVALS**
PASSAPORTES	**PASSPORT CONTROL**
CIDADÃOS DA CEE	**EC PASSPORT HOLDERS**
RECOLHA DE BAGAGEM	**BAGGAGE RECLAIM**
ALFÂNDEGA	**CUSTOMS CONTROL**
NADA A DECLARAR	**NOTHING TO DECLARE**
ARTIGOS A DECLARAR	**ARTICLES TO DECLARE**
SAIDA	**EXIT**
WC	**TOILETS**
PONTO DE ENCONTRO	**MEETING POINT**
TRANSFERÊNCIAS	**TRANSFER**
TRÂNSITOS	**TRANSIT**

Where is the luggage for the flight from...?
Onde está a bagagem do voo de...?
***on**duh shta uh ba**gah**-jayñ doo **voh**-oo duh...*

Where can I change some money?
Onde posso trocar dinheiro?
***on**duh **poss**oo troo**kar** deen-**yay**-roo*

How do I/we get to the centre of *(name town)***...?**
Como se vai para o centro de...?
***koh**-moo suh vy **pa**ruh oo **sen**troo duh...*

How much is the taxi fare...? | **into town** | **to the hotel**
Quanto custa ir de táxi...? | para o centro | para o hotel
kwan**too **koosh**tuh eer duh **ta**xee...* | ***pa**ruh oo **sen**troo* | *pro oh-**tel

Is there a bus to the city centre?
Há algum autocarro para o centro?
*a al**gooñ** owtoo-**kar**roo **pa**ruh oo **sen**troo*

■ BUS ■ LUGGAGE ■ METRO ■ TAXI

PARTIDAS	DEPARTURES		
CARTÃO DE EMBARQUE	BOARDING CARD	VOO	FLIGHT
PORTA DE EMBARQUE	BOARDING GATE	ATRASO	DELAY

Where do I check in for the flight to...?
Onde faço o check-in para o voo de...?
onduh fah-soo oo check-in paruh oo voh-oo duh...

Which is the departure gate for the flight to...?
Qual é a porta de embarque do voo para...?
kwal e uh portuh duh embar-k doo voh-oo paruh...

■ YOU MAY HEAR

O embarque será na porta número...
oo embar-k suh-rah nuh portuh noomeroo...
Boarding will take place at gate number...

Última chamada para os passageiros do voo...
ooltimuh shamah-duh paruh oosh passuh-jay-roosh doo voh-oo...
Last call for passengers on flight...

O seu voo está atrasado
oo sayoo voh-oo shta atruh-zah-doo
Your flight is delayed

■ IF YOU NEED TO CHANGE OR CHECK ON YOUR FLIGHT

I want to change / cancel my reservation
Quero mudar / cancelar a minha reserva
kehroo moodar / kansuh-lar uh meen-yuh ruh-zehrvuh

I'd like to reconfirm my flight to...
Gostaria de confirmar o meu voo para...
gooshtuh-ree-uh duh komfeermar oo mayoo voh-oo paruh...

Is the flight to ... delayed?
O voo para ... está atrasado?
oo voh-oo paruh ... shta atruh-zah-doo

The Portuguese alphabet is the same as the English one, with the exception of the three letters: K, W and Y. These letters are only used in foreign words that have come into use in Portuguese.

How do you spell it?	**C as in Carlos, L as in Lisboa**
Como se escreve?	C de Carlos, L de Lisboa
***koh**-moo suh shkrev*	*say duh **kar**loosh el duh leej**boh**-uh*

A	*a*	**Alexandre**	*aluh-**shan**druh*
B	*bay*	**Bastos**	***bash**-toosh*
C	*say*	**Carlos**	***kar**loosh*
D	*day*	**Daniel**	*dan-**yel***
E	*ay*	**Eduardo**	*eed**war**doo*
F	*ef*	**França**	***fran**suh*
G	*jay*	**Gabriel**	*gabree-**el***
H	*a**ga***	**Holanda**	*oh-**lan**duh*
I	*ee*	**Itália**	*ee**tal**-yuh*
J	***jot**uh*	**José**	*joo**ze***
L	*el*	**Lisboa**	*leej**boh**-uh*
M	*em*	**Maria**	*ma**ree**-uh*
N	*en*	**Nicolau**	*neekoo-**la**-oo*
O	*oh*	**Oscar**	***osh**kar*
P	*pay*	**Paris**	*pa**reesh***
Q	*kay*	**Quarto**	***kwar**too*
R	*err*	**Ricardo**	*ree**kar**doo*
S	*ess*	**Susana**	*soo**zan**uh*
T	*tay*	**Teresa**	*tuh-**ray**-zuh*
U	*oo*	**Ulisses**	*oo**lee**sush*
V	*vay*	**Venezuela**	*vuh-nuh-**zway**-luh*
X	*sheesh*	**Xangai**	*shang-**gye***
Z	*zay*	**Zebra**	***ze**bruh*

Yes
Sim
seeñ

No
Não
nowñ

Please
Por favor / Faz favor / Se faz favor
*poor fa**vor** / fash fa**vor** / suh fash fa**vor***

Thank you
Obrigado / Obrigada *(fem.)*
*oh-bree**gah**-doo / oh-bree**gah**-duh*

Thanks very much
Muito obrigado(a)
***mween**too oh-bree**gah**-doo(uh)*

OK!
Está bem
shta bayñ

Don't mention it
De nada
*duh **nah**-duh*

With pleasure!
Com muito prazer!
*koñ **mween**too pra**zehr***

Sir / Mr
Senhor / Sr.
*sun-**yor***

Madam / Mrs / Ms
Senhora / Sra.
*sun-**yor**uh*

Miss
Menina
*muh-**nee**nuh*

Excuse me! *(to catch attention)*
Por favor!
*poor fa**vor***

Excuse me *(sorry)*
Desculpe
*dush**koolp***

Pardon?
Como?
***koh**-moo*

I don't know
Não sei
nowñ say

I don't understand
Não compreendo
*nowñ kompree-**en**doo*

Do you understand?
Compreende?
*kompree-**en**duh*

Do you speak English?
Fala inglês?
fah**-luh een**glesh

Could you repeat that, please?
Pode repetir, por favor?
*pod ruhpuh**teer** poor fa**vor***

Do you have...?
Tem...?
tayñ...

I'd like...
Queria...
***kree**-uh...*

We'd like...
Queríamos...
***kree**-uhmoosh...*

How much is...?
Quanto custa...?
***kwan**too **koosh**tuh...*

this
isto
***eesh**too*

that
isso
***ess**oo*

Where is...?
Onde está...?
***on**duh shta...*

When do you close?
Quando fecha?
***kwan**doo **fay**shuh*

CROSSING	**A TRAVESSIA**
CRUISE	**O CRUZEIRO**
CABIN	**O CAMAROTE**

When is the next boat to...?
Quando parte o próxima barco para...?
__kwan__doo part oo __pross__imoo __bar__koo __pa__ruh...

Have you a timetable?
Tem um horário?
tayñ ooñ oh-__rar__-yoo

Is there a car ferry to...?
Há um ferry-boat para...?
a ooñ ferry-boat __pa__ruh...

How much is a ticket...?
Quanto é o bilhete...?
__kwan__too e oo beel-__yet__...

single
de ida
__dee__duh

return
de ida e volta
__dee__duh ee __vol__tuh

A tourist ticket
Um bilhete de segunda classe
ooñ beel-__yet__ duh se__goon__duh klass

How much is the crossing for a car and ... people?
Quanto é a passagem para ... pessoas e um carro?
__kwan__too e uh pa__sah__-jayñ __pa__ruh ... puh-__so__-ush ee ooñ __kar__roo

How long is the journey?
Quanto dura a viagem?
__kwan__to __doo__ruh vee-__ah__-jayñ

What time do we get to...?
A que horas chegamos a...?
uh kee __or__ush shuh__gah__-moosh uh...

Where does the boat leave from?
De onde parte o barco?
dee__on__duh part oo __bar__koo

When is...?
A que horas é...?
uh kee __or__uz e...

the first boat
o primeiro barco
oo pree__may__-roo __bar__koo

the last boat?
o último barco
oo __ool__timoo __bar__koo

Is there somewhere to eat on the boat?
O barco tem restaurante?
oo __bar__koo tayñ rushtoh-__rant__

In Portuguese the possessive (my, his, her, etc) is generally not used with parts of the body, e.g.

My head hurts	***Doi-me a cabeça***
My hands are dirty	***Tenho as mãos sujas***

ankle	**o tornozelo**	*toornoo-**zel**oo*
arm	**o braço**	***brah**-soo*
back	**as costas**	***kosh**tush*
bone	**o osso**	***oss**oo*
chin	**o queixo**	***kay**-shoo*
ear	**a orelha / o ouvido**	*oh-**rel**-yuh / oh-**vee**doo*
elbow	**o cotovelo**	*kootoo-**vel**oo*
eye	**o olho**	***ohl**-yoo*
finger	**o dedo**	***deh**-doo*
foot	**o pé**	*pe*
hair	**o cabelo**	*ka**bay**-loo*
hand	**a mão**	*mowñ*
head	**a cabeça**	*ka**beh**-suh*
heart	**o coração**	*kooruh-**sowñ***
hip	**a anca**	***an**-kuh*
joint	**a articulação**	*arteekoo-la**sowñ***
kidney	**o rim**	*reeñ*
knee	**o joelho**	***jwel**-yoo*
leg	**a perna**	***pehr**nuh*
liver	**o fígado**	***fee**guh-doo*
mouth	**a boca**	***boh**-kuh*
nail	**a unha**	***oon**-yuh*
neck	**o pescoço**	*push-**koh**-soo*
nose	**o nariz**	*na**reesh***
stomach	**o estômago**	***shtoh**-magoo*
throat	**a garganta**	*gar**gan**tuh*
thumb	**o polegar**	*poh-luh-**gar***
toe	**o dedo do pé**	***deh**-doo doo pe*
wrist	**o pulso**	***pool**-soo*

■ DOCTOR ■ PHARMACY

Can you help me?
Pode-me ajudar?
__pod__-muh ajoo__dar__

My car has broken down
Tenho o carro avariado
__ten__yoo oo __kar__roo avuh-ree-__ah__-doo

The car won't start
O carro não pega
oo __kar__roo nowñ __peh__-guh

The battery is flat
A bateria está descarregada
uh batuh-__ree__-uh shta dushkarray-__gah__-duh

I've run out of petrol
Não tenho gasolina
nowñ __ten__-yoo gazoo-__lee__nuh

Is there a garage near here?
Há alguma garagem por aqui?
a al__goo__muh ga__rah__-jayñ poor a__kee__

The engine is overheating
O motor está a aquecer demais
oo moo__tor__ shta akuh-__sehr__ duh-__mysh__

I need water
Preciso de água
pre-__see__zoo __dahg__-wuh

It's leaking...	**petrol**	**oil**	**water**
Está a perder...	gasolina	óleo	água
shta uh per__dehr__...	*gazoo-__lee__nuh*	*__ol__-yoo*	*__ahg__-wuh*

I've a flat tyre
Tenho um furo
__ten__-yoo ooñ __foo__roo

I can't get the wheel off
Não consigo tirar a roda
nowñ kon__see__goo tee__rar__ uh __rod__uh

Can you tow me to the nearest garage?
Pode-me rebocar até à oficina mais próxima?
__pod__-muh ruh-boo__kar__ a__te__ a ofee-__see__-nuh mysh __pross__imuh

Do you have parts for a (*make of car*)**...?**
Tem peças para um...?
tayñ __pess__ush __pa__ruh ooñ...

The ... doesn't work properly *(see* CAR–PARTS*)*
O/A ... não funciona bem
oo/uh ... nowñ foonss-__yo__nuh bayñ

Can you replace the windscreen?
Pode substituir o pára-brisas?
pod soobshtee-__tweer__ oo __pa__ruh-__bree__zush

■ CAR–PARTS

If you intend using buses a lot, it is worth enquiring at the Tourist Office how to get hold of a travel pass – **um passe***. The word for both bus and coach is* **o autocarro***.*

Is there a bus to...?
Há autocarro para...?
*a owtoo-**karr**oo **pa**ruh...*

Which bus goes to...?
Que autocarro vai a...?
*kuh owtoo-**karr**oo vy uh...*

Where do I catch the bus to...?
Onde apanho um autocarro para...?
***on**duh apan-**yoo** ooñ owtoo-**karr**oo **pa**ruh...*

We're going to...
Vamos para...
***vuh**-moosh **pa**ruh...*

Where do they sell bus tickets?
Onde vendem módulos / bilhetes?
***on**duh ven**dayñ** **moh**-doo-loosh / beel-**yet**sh*

How much is it...?
Quanto é...?
***kwan**too e...*

to the centre
para o centro
***pa**ruh oo **sen**troo*

to the beach
para a praia
***pa**ruh uh **pry**-uh*

to Sintra
para Sintra
***pa**ruh **seen**tra*

How often are the buses to...?
Que frequência têm os autocarros para...?
*kuh fruh-**kwens**yuh tay-**ayñ** oosh owtoo-**karr**oosh **pa**ruh...*

When is the first / the last bus to...?
A que horas é o primeiro / o último autocarro para...?
*uh kee **or**uz e oo pree**may**-roo / oo **ool**timoo owtoo-**karr**oo **pa**ruh...*

Please tell me when to get off
Pode-me dizer quando devo sair?
pod**-muh dee**zehr** **kwan**doo **deh**-voo suh-**eer

This is my stop
Esta é a minha paragem
***esh**-tuh e uh **meen**-yuh pa**rah**-jayñ*

■ YOU MAY HEAR

Este autocarro não pára em...
*aysht owtoo-**karr**oo nowñ **pah**-ruh ayñ...*
This bus doesn't stop in...

Tem que apanhar o...
*tayñ kuh apan-**yar** oo...*
You must catch the...

■ METRO ■ TAXI

BOARD MEETING	A REUNIÃO DO CONSELHO DE ADMINISTRAÇÃO
CONFERENCE ROOM	A SALA DE CONFERÊNCIAS
MEETING ROOM	A SALA DE REUNIÕES
MANAGING DIRECTOR	O DIRECTOR GERAL / A DIRECTORA GERAL
MEETING	A REUNIÃO
MINUTES	AS MINUTAS
SAMPLE	A MOSTRA
TO DRAW UP A CONTRACT	REDIGIR UM CONTRATO
TRADE FAIR	A FEIRA DE MOSTRAS
TURNOVER	O VOLUME DE VENDAS

I'd like to arrange a meeting with...
Gostaria de ter uma reunião com...
*gooshtuh-**ree**-uh duh tehr **oom**uh ree-oo-**nyowñ** koñ...*

Can we meet...?
Podemos encontrar-nos...?
*poo**deh**-moosh anykon-**trar**-noosh...*

for lunch
para almoçar
pa**ruh almoo**sar

for dinner
para jantar
pa**ruh jan**tar

on the 4th of May at 1100
no dia quatro de Maio às onze
*noo **dee**-uh **kwa**troo duh **my**-oo ush onz*

I will confirm...
Confirmarei...
*komfeer-ma**ray**...*

by letter
por carta
*poor **kar**tuh*

by fax
por fax
poor fax

How do I get to your office?
Como se vai ao seu escritório?
***koh**-moo suh vy ow **say**oo shkree-**tor**-yoo*

I'm staying at Hotel...
Estou no Hotel...
*sh**to** noo oh-**tel**...*

Please let ... know that I will be ... minutes late
Por favor avise ... que chegarei com um atraso de ... minutos
*poor fa**vor** a-**vee**-zuh ... kuh shuh-ga**ray** koñ ooñ a**trah**-zoo duh ... mee**noo**toosh*

I'm very sorry but I won't be able to see ..., as arranged
Lamento muito mas não posso ver ..., conforme combinado
*la**men**-too **mween**too mush nowñ **poss**oo vehr ... kon**form** kombee-**nah**-doo*

May I leave a message?
Posso deixar um recado?
possoo dayshar ooñ rekah-doo

I have an appointment with...
Tenho um encontro com...
ten-yoo ooñ ayñ-kontroo koñ...

at ... o'clock
às ... horas
ush ... orush

Here is my card
Aqui tem o meu cartão
akee tayñ oo mayoo kartowñ

I'm delighted to meet you at last
É um prazer encontrá-lo(-la) finalmente
e ooñ prazehr ayñ-kontrah-loo(-luh) feenalment

I don't know much Portuguese
Não sei muito português
nowñ say mweentoo poortoo-gesh

Can you speak more slowly
Pode falar mais devagar
pod falar mysh devuhgar

I'm sorry I'm late
Desculpe chegar tarde
dushkoolp shuhgar tard

My flight was delayed
O avião veio atrasado
oo av-yowñ vayoo atruh-zah-doo

May I introduce you to...
Posso-lhe apresentar...
possoo-lyuh apruhzen-tar...

■ YOU MAY HEAR

Tem encontro marcado?
tayñ ayñ-kontroo markah-doo
Do you have an appointment?

Ele / Ela não vem hoje
ayl / eluh nowñ vayñ ohj
He/She isn't coming in today

O Senhor... não está
oo sun-yor... nowñ shta
Senhor... isn't in

Está...
shta...
He is...

de férias
duh fehr-yush
on holiday

de viagem
duh vee-ah-jayñ
travelling

Volta dentro de cinco minutos
voltuh dentroo duh seenkoo meenootosh
He / She will be back in five minutes

■ FAX ■ LETTERS ■ OFFICE ■ TELEPHONE

Local tourist offices should have ***uma lista de parques de campismo*** *with prices.*

Do you have a list of campsites with prices?
Tem uma lista de parques de campismo com os preços?
*tayñ **oom**uh **leesh**tuh duh parksh duh kam**peej**moo koñ oosh **pray**-soosh*

How far is the beach?
A que distância é a praia?
*uh kuh deesh-**tanss**-yuh e uh **pry**-uh*

Is there a restaurant on the campsite?
Há algum restaurante no parque?
*a al**gooñ** rushtoh-**rant** noo park*

Have you places?
Tem vagas?
*tayñ **vah**-gush*

We'd like to stay for ... nights
Gostariamos de ficar ... noites
*gooshtuh-**ree**-uhmoosh duh fee**kar** ... noytsh*

How much is it per night...?
Quanto é por noite...?
***kwan**too e poor noyt...*

for a tent
por tenda
*poor **ten**duh*

per person
por pessoa
*poor puh-**so**-uh*

Are showers...
Os duches...
*oosh **doosh**ush...*

Is hot water...
A água quente...
*uh **ahg**-wuh kent...*

Is electricity...
A electricidade...
*uh eeletree-see**dahd**...*

...included in the price?
...são incluidos no preço?
*...sowñ een-**klwee**doosh noo **pray**-soo*

Can we camp here overnight? *(for tent)*
Podemos acampar aqui para passar a noite?
*poo**deh**-mooz akam**par** a**kee** **pa**ruh pa**ssar** uh noyt*

Can we park the caravan / trailer here?
Podemos estacionar a caravana / roulotte aqui?
*poo**deh**-moosh shtass-yoo**nar** uh karuh-**vah**-nuh / roo**lot** akee*

Is good drinking water available?
Há boa água potável?
*a **boh**-uh **ahg**-wuh poo**tah**-vel*

■ SIGHTSEEING & TOURIST OFFICE

Parking spaces may be free and car parks vary. You will have to ask about payment and length of stay. A restricted parking area is called a ***zona azul****.*

AUTO-ESTRADA	**MOTORWAY** *(signs are in blue)*
CENTRO DA CIDADE	**CITY CENTRE**
CIRCUNVALAÇÃO	**BYPASS**
CIRCULE PELA DIREITA	**KEEP RIGHT**
CURVA PERIGOSA	**DANGEROUS BEND**
DÊ PRIORIDADE	**GIVE WAY**
DEVAGAR	**SLOW DOWN**
ESTACIONAMENTO	**PARKING**
ESTACIONAMENTO PROIBIDO	**NO PARKING**
PORTAGEM	**TOLL**
SENTIDO ÚNICO	**ONE-WAY STREET**
VEDADO AO TRÂNSITO	**ROAD CLOSED**
VEÍCULOS PESADOS	**HEAVY VEHICLES**
VELOCIDADE MÁXIMA	**SPEED LIMIT**

Can I/we park here?
Pode-se estacionar aqui?
__pod__-suh shtass-yoo__nar__ a__kee__

How long for?
Por quanto tempo?
poor __kwan__too __tem__poo

Do I/we need a parking ticket?
É preciso um bilhete?
e pre-__see__zoo ooñ beel-__yet__

We're going to...
Vamos a...
__vuh__-moosh uh...

What is the best route?
Qual é o melhor caminho?
kwal e oo mul-__yor__ ka__meen__-yoo

Will the motorway be busy?
Haverá muito tráfego na auto-estrada
uhv__rah__ __mween__too __trah__-fuh-goo nuh owtoo-__shtrah__-duh

■ BREAKDOWNS ■ PETROL STATION

DRIVING LICENCE	A CARTA DE CONDUÇÃO
FULLY COMPREHENSIVE INSURANCE	O SEGURO CONTRA TODOS OS RISCOS
REVERSE GEAR	A MARCHA ATRÁS

I want to hire a car
Queria alugar um carro
__kree__-uh aloo__gar__ ooñ __kar__roo

for ... days
para ... dias
__pa__ruh ... __dee__-ush

the weekend
o fim-de-semana
oo feeñ du se__mah__-nuh

What are your rates...?
Quais são as tarifas...?
kwaysh sowñ ush tuh-__ree__-fush...

per day
por dia
poor __dee__-uh

per week
por semana
poor se__mah__-nuh

How much is the deposit?
Quanto deixo de sinal?
__kwan__too __day__-shoo duh see__nal__

Is there a kilometre charge?
Paga-se quilometragem?
__pah__-guh-suh keelome__trah__-jayñ

Is fully comprehensive insurance included?
Inclui o seguro contra todos os riscos?
een-__klwee__ oo se__goo__roo __kon__truh __toh__-duz oosh __reesh__koosh

Do I have to return the car here?
Tenho que devolver o carro aqui?
__ten__-yoo kuh duh-vol__vehr__ oo __kar__roo a__kee__

By what time?
A que horas?
uh kuh __or__ush

I'd like to leave it in...
Gostaria de o deixar em...
gooshtuh-__ree__-uh duh oo day__shar__ ayñ...

What shall I do if the car breaks down?
Que devo fazer se o carro se avariar?
kuh __deh__-voo fa__zehr__ suh oo __kar__roo suh avuhree-__yar__

How can I get in touch with you, if needed?
Como devo entrar em contacto, se necessário?
__koh__-moo __deh__-voo ayn__trar__ ayñ kon__tak__too suh nussuh-__sar__-yoo

■ **YOU MAY HEAR**

Por favor devolva o carro com o depósito cheio
poor fa__vor__ duh-__vol__vuh oo __kar__roo koñ oo duh-__poz__itoo __shay__oo
Please return the car with a full tank

The ... doesn't work	**The ... don't work**
O/A ... não funciona	**Os/As ... não funcionam**
*oo/uh ... nowñ foonss-**yo**nuh*	*oosh/ush ... nowñ foonss-**yo**nowñ*

accelerator	**o acelerador**	*assuh-luh-ra**dor***
battery	**a bateria**	*batuh-**ree**-uh*
bonnet	**o capot**	*kah-**po***
brakes	**os travões**	*tra**voynsh***
choke	**o motor de arranque**	*moo**tor** dee a**rrank***
clutch	**a embraiagem**	*ayñ-bry-**ah**-jayñ*
distributor	**o distribuidor**	*deesh-tree-bwee-**dor***
engine	**o motor**	*moo**tor***
exhaust pipe	**o tubo de escape**	***too**boo dush**kap***
fuse	**o fusível**	*foo**zee**vel*
gears	**as mudanças**	*moo**dan**sush*
handbrake	**o travão de mão**	*tra**vowñ** duh mowñ*
headlights	**os farois**	*fa**roysh***
ignition	**a ignição**	*eegnee-**sowñ***
indicator	**o indicador**	*eendeekuh**dor***
points	**os platinados**	*platee-**nah**-doosh*
radiator	**o radiador**	*radee-uh-**dor***
rear lights	**os pilotos traseiros**	*pee**lo**toosh tra**zay**roosh*
seat belt	**o cinto de segurança**	***seen**too duh segoo**ran**-suh*
spare wheel	**a roda sobressalente**	***ro**duh sobruh-sa**lent***
spark plugs	**as velas**	***vel**ush*
steering	**a direcção**	*deere**sowñ***
steering wheel	**o volante**	*voo**lant***
tyre	**o pneu**	***pnay**-oo*
wheel	**a roda**	***ro**duh*
windscreen	**o pára-brisas**	***pa**ruh-**bree**zush*
-- washer	**o lava pára-brisas**	***la**vuh **pa**ruh-**bree**zush*
-- wiper	**o limpa pára-brisas**	***leem**puh **pa**ruh-**bree**zush*

■ BREAKDOWNS ■ PETROL STATION

My best wishes for a...
Os meus votos de...
*oosh **may**oosh **vot**oosh duh...*

I'd like to wish you a... *(familiar)*
Desejo que tenhas um...
*duh-**zay**-joo kuh **ten**-yush ooñ...*

Merry Christmas!
Bom Natal!
*boñ na**tal***

Happy New Year!
Feliz Ano Novo!
*fuh-**leesh ah**-noo **noh**-voo*

Happy birthday!
Feliz aniversário!
*fuh-**leesh** aneever-**sar**-yoo*

Have a good trip!
Muito boa viagem!
***mween**too **boh**-uh vee-**ah**-jayñ*

Best wishes!
Felicidades!
*feleesee-**dah**-dush*

Welcome!
Bem-vindo(a)!
*bayñ-**veen**-doo(uh)*

Enjoy your meal!
Bom apetite!
*boñ apuh-**teet***

Thanks, and you too!
Obrigado(a), igualmente!
*oh-bree**gah**-doo(uh) eegwal**ment***

Cheers!
Saúde!
*sa-**ood***

Congratulations! *(having a baby, getting married, etc)*
Parabéns!
*paruh-**baynsh***

■ LETTERS ■ MAKING FRIENDS

In Portugal it is customary to show films in their original versions, with subtitles. For English-speaking visitors this is a good thing, as most films are in English.

PARA MAIORES DE 18 ANOS	FOR PERSONS OVER 18
SESSÃO	PERFORMANCE

What's on at the cinema?
Qual é o programa no cinema?
*kwal e oo proo**grah**-muh noo see**nay**-muh*

When does *(name film)* **start?**
A que horas começa ...?
*uh kee **or**ush koo**mess**uh...*

How much are the tickets?
Quanto custam os bilhetes?
kwan**too koosh**towñ** oosh beel-**yetsh

Two for the *(time)* **showing**
Dois para a sessão das...
*doysh pra suh**sowñ** dush...*

What films have you seen recently?
Que filmes viu ultimamente?
*kuh **feel**mush vyoo ooltimuh**ment***

What is *(English name of film)* **called in Portuguese?**
Como se chama ... em português?
koh**-moo suh **sha**mah ... ayñ poortoo-**gesh

Who is your favourite actor / actress?
De que actor / actriz gosta mais?
*duh kee a**tor** / a**treesh gosh**tuh mysh*

■ YOU MAY HEAR

Para a sala um / dois não temos lugares
***pa**ruh uh **sah**-luh ooñ / doysh nowñ **teh**-moosh loo**ga**rush*
For screen 1 / 2 we have no tickets left

■ ENTERTAINMENT ■ LEISURE/INTERESTS

*Size for clothes is **a medida** . Size for shoes is **o número***

women

sizes	
UK	EC
10	36
12	38
14	40
16	42
18	44
20	46

men - suits

sizes	
UK	EC
36	46
38	48
40	50
42	52
44	54
46	56

shoes

sizes			
UK	EC	UK	EC
2	35	8	42
3	36	9	43
4	37	10	44
5	38	11	45
6	39		
7	41		

May I try this on?
Posso provar isto?
***poss**oo proo**var eesh**too*

Where are the changing rooms?
Onde é o gabinete de provas?
***on**duh e oo gabee**net** duh **prov**ush*

Have you a size...?
Tem uma medida...?
*tayñ **oom**uh muh**dee**-duh...*

bigger
maior
*ma**yor***

smaller
mais pequena
*mysh puh-**kay**nuh*

Have you this...?
Tem isto...?
*tayñ **eesh**too...*

in my size
na minha medida
*nuh **meen**-yuh muh**dee**-duh*

in other colours
em outras cores
*ayñ **oh**-trush **ko**rush*

That's a shame!
Que pena!
*kuh **pay**nuh*

It's too...
É muito...
*e **mween**too...*

short
curto
***koor**too*

long
comprido
*kom**pree**doo*

I'm just looking
Só estou a ver
so shtoh uh vehr

I'll take it
Quero comprar
kehr**oo kom**prar

■ **YOU MAY HEAR**

De que medida?
*duh kuh muh**dee**-duh*
What size?

Quer provar?
*kehr proo**var***
Do you want to try it on?

Fica bem?
***fee**kuh bayñ*
Does it fit?

■ NUMBERS ■ PAYING ■ SHOPPING

COTTON	O ALGODÃO	SILK	A SEDA
LACE	A RENDA	SUEDE	A CAMURÇA
LEATHER	O COURO	WOOL	A LÃ

belt	**o cinto**	***seen**too*
blouse	**a blusa**	***bloo**zuh*
bra	**o soutien**	*soot-**yañ***
coat	**o casaco**	*ka**zah**-koo*
dress	**o vestido**	*vush**tee**doo*
gloves	**as luvas**	***loo**vush*
hat	**o chapéu**	*sha**pay**-oo*
hat *(woollen)*	**a boina**	***boy**nuh*
jacket	**o casaco curto**	*ka**zah**-koo **koor**too*
knickers	**as cuecas**	***kwe**kush*
nightdress	**a camisa de dormir**	*ka**mee**zuh duh door**meer***
pyjamas	**o pijama**	*pee**jah**-muh*
raincoat	**o impermeável**	*eempermee-**ah**-vel*
sandals	**as sandálias**	*san**dahl**-yush*
scarf *(silk)*	**o lenço**	***len**soo*
scarf *(wool)*	**o cachecol**	*kashu-**kol***
shirt	**a camisa**	*ka**mee**zuh*
shorts	**os calções**	*kal**soynsh***
skirt	**a saia**	***sy**-uh*
slippers	**as chinelas**	*shee**ne**lush*
socks	**as peúgas**	***pew**-gush*
suit	**o fato**	***fah**-too*
swimsuit	**o fato de banho**	***fah**-too duh **bahn**-yoo*
tie	**a gravata**	*gruh-**vah**-tuh*
tights	**os collants**	*ko**lansh***
tracksuit	**o fato de treino**	***fah**-too duh **tray**-noo*
trousers	**as calças**	***kal**sush*
t-shirt	**a camisola**	*kuhmee**zoh**-luh*
underpants	**as cuecas**	***kwe**kush*
zip	**o fecho éclair**	***fay**-shoo ay-**klehr***

> *Two key words for describing colours in Portuguese are:*
> ***claro*** *light* ***escuro*** *dark*

black	**preto(a)**	***pray**-too(uh)*
blue	**azul**	*a**zool***
navy blue	**azul escuro**	*a**zool shkoo**roo*
brown	**castanho(a)**	*kash**tahn**-yoo(uh)*
cream	**bege**	*behj*
crimson	**carmesim**	*karmuh-**zeeñ***
gold	**dourado(a)**	*dough-**rah**doo(uh)*
green	**verde**	*vehrd*
grey	**cinzento(a)**	*seen-**zen**too(uh)*
orange	**cor de laranja**	*kor duh la**ran**juh*
pink	**cor de rosa**	*kor duh **roh**zuh*
purple	**roxo(a)**	***roh**-shoo(uh)*
red	**encarnado(a) /**	*aynkar**nah**-doo(uh)*
	vermelho(a)	*ver**mel**-yoo(uh)*
silver	**prateado(a)**	*prat-**yah**-doo*
turquoise	**azul turquesa**	*a**zool** toor**keh**-zuh*
white	**branco(a)**	***bran**koo(uh)*
yellow	**amarelo(a)**	*amuh-**rel**oo(uh)*

■ SHAPE

big	**grande**	*grand*
fat	**gordo(a)**	***gor**doo(uh)*
flat	**plano(a)**	***plah**-noo(uh)*
long	**comprido(a)**	*kom**pree**doo(uh)*
narrow	**estreito(a)**	***shtray**-too(uh)*
round	**redondo(a)**	*ruh-**don**doo(uh)*
small	**pequeno(a)**	*puh-**kay**-noo(uh)*
square	**quadrado(a)**	*kwa**drah**-doo(uh)*
tall	**alto(a)**	***al**too(uh)*
thick	**grosso(a)**	***gross**oo(uh)*
thin	**magro(a)**	***mah**-groo(uh)*
tiny	**pequenino(a)**	*puh-kay**nee**noo(uh)*
wide	**largo(a)**	***lar**goo(uh)*

This doesn't work
Isto não trabalha
eeshto nowñ trabal-yuh

This is out of order
Isto não funciona
eeshto nowñ foonss-yonuh

The ... doesn't work
O/A ... não trabalha
oo/uh ... nowñ trabal-yuh

The ... are out of order
Os/As ... não funcionam
oosh/ush ... nowñ foonss-yonowñ

light
a luz
uh loosh

heating
o aquecimento
oo akuhsee-mentoo

air conditioning
o ar condicionado
oo ar kondeess-yoonah-doo

There's a problem with the room
Há um problema com o quarto
a ooñ proo-blemuh koñ oo kwartoo

It's noisy
Há muito barulho
a mweentoo barool-yoo

It's too hot *(room)*
É muito quente
e mweentoo kent

It's too cold *(room)*
É muito frio
e mweentoo free-oo

It's too hot / cold *(food)*
Está muito quente / frio
shta mweentoo kent / free-oo

The meat is cold
A carne está fria
uh karn shta free-uh

This isn't what I ordered
Isto não é o que eu pedi
eeshtoo nowñ e oo kuh ay-oo puh-dee

To whom should I complain?
A quem me posso queixar?
uh kayñ muh possoo kayshar

It's faulty
Tem um defeito
tayñ ooñ duh-fay-too

I want a refund
Quero um reembolso
kehroo ooñ ree-aym-bolsoo

I want to return it
Quero devolver
kehroo duh-volvehr

The goods were damaged in transit
A mercadoria ficou danificada no caminho
uh merka-dooreeuh feekoh duhnee-feekah-duh noo kameen-yoo

■ PROBLEMS ■ REPAIRS ■ ROOM SERVICE

COMPUTER	O COMPUTADOR
DATABASE	O BANCO DE DADOS
FILE	O FICHEIRO
FLOPPY DISK	O DISQUETE
HARD DISK	O DISCO DURO
KEYBOARD	O TECLADO
SCREEN	O ECRÃ

What computer do you use?
Que computador usa?
*kuh kompootuh-**dor** **oo**zuh*

Is it IBM compatible?
É compatível com IBM?
*e kompa-**tee**-vel koñ IBM*

Do you have E-mail?
Tem correio electrónico?
*tayñ koo**ray**oo eele**tron**ikoo*

What is your address?
Qual é a sua morada?
*kwal e uh **soo**-uh moo**rah**-duh*

Do you have a database?
Tem banco de dados?
*tayñ **ban**koo duh **dah**-doosh*

How often do you update it?
Quando o actualiza?
***kwan**doo oo atwa-**lee**zuh*

Can you send it on a floppy disk?
Pode-me mandar isso em disquete?
pod**-muh man**dar** **ees**soo ayñ deesh**ket

What word processing package do you use?
Que processador de textos usa?
*kuh proo-suh-sa-**dor** duh **tesh**toosh **oo**zuh*

How much memory does the computer have?
Que capacidade de memória tem o computador?
*kuh ka-puh-see**dahd** duh me**mor**-ya tayñ oo **say**oo kompootuh-**dor***

■ OFFICE

With the single European Market, EC citizens are subject only to highly selective spot checks and they can go through the blue customs channel (unless they have goods to declare). There is no restriction, either by quantity or value, on goods purchased by travellers in another EC country provided they are ***for their own personal use*** *(guidelines have been published). If you are unsure of certain items, check with the customs officials as to whether payment of duty is required.*

CONTROLE DE PASSAPORTES	PASSPORT CONTROL
CEE	EC
CARTEIRA DE IDENTIDADE	NATIONAL IDENTITY DOCUMENT
ALFÂNDEGA	CUSTOMS

Do I have to pay duty on this?
É preciso pagar direitos para isto?
*e pre-**see**zoo pa**gar** dee**ray**-toosh **pa**ruh **eesh**too*

I bought this as a gift
Comprei para oferecer
*kom**pray** **pa**ruh of-fuh-ruh-**sehr***

It is for my own personal use
É para meu uso pessoal
*e **pa**ruh **may**oo **oo**zoo puh-**swal***

We are in transit
Estamos aqui em trânsito
***shta**moosh a**kee** ayñ **tran**zitoo*

We are going to...
Vamos a...
***vuh**-moosh uh...*

The children are on this passport
As crianças estão neste passaporte
*ush kree-**an**sush shtowñ nesht passuh-**port***

days

MONDAY	SEGUNDA-FEIRA
TUESDAY	TERÇA-FEIRA
WEDNESDAY	QUARTA-FEIRA
THURSDAY	QUINTA-FEIRA
FRIDAY	SEXTA-FEIRA
SATURDAY	SÁBADO
SUNDAY	DOMINGO

seasons

SPRING	A PRIMAVERA
SUMMER	O VERÃO
AUTUMN	O OUTONO
WINTER	O INVERNO

months

JANUARY	JANEIRO
FEBRUARY	FEVEREIRO
MARCH	MARÇO
APRIL	ABRIL
MAY	MAIO
JUNE	JUNHO
JULY	JULHO
AUGUST	AGOSTO
SEPTEMBER	SETEMBRO
OCTOBER	OUTUBRO
NOVEMBER	NOVEMBRO
DECEMBER	DEZEMBRO

What is today's date?
Qual é a data hoje?
*kwal e uh **dah**-tuh ohj*

What day is it today?
Que dia é hoje?
*kuh **dee**-uh e ohj*

It's the 5th of May 1995
É cinco de Maio de mil novecentos e noventa e cinco
*e **seen**koo duh **my**-oo duh meel nov**sen**toosh ee noo**ven**tuh ee **seen**koo*

on Saturday
no sábado
*noo **sa**badoo*

on Saturdays
aos sábados
*awsh **sa**badoosh*

every Saturday
todos os sábados
*toh-**doosh** oosh **sa**badoosh*

this Saturday
este sábado
*esht **sa**badoo*

next Saturday
o próximo sábado
*oo **pross**imoo **sa**badoo*

last Saturday
o sábado passado
*oo **sa**badoo puh-**sah**doo*

in June
em Junho
*ayñ **joon**-yoo*

at the beginning of...
no princípio de...
*noo preen-**seep**-yoo duh...*

at the end of...
no fim de...
noo feeñ duh...

before the summer
antes do verão
*antsh doo vuh-**rowñ***

during the summer
durante o verão
*doo**rant** oo vuh-**rowñ***

after the summer
depois do verão
*duh-**poysh** doo vuh-**rowñ***

■ NUMBERS

FILLING	**O CHUMBO**
CROWN	**A COROA**
DENTURES	**A DENTADURA POS**
A TEMPORARY REPAIR	**UM TRATAMENTO P**

I need a dentist
Preciso de um dentista
*pre-**see**zoo dooñ den**teesh**tuh*

I have too
Tenho uma
ten**-yoo **oom

Can you do a temporary filling?
Pode pôr um chumbo provisório?
*pod por ooñ **shoom**boo provee-**zor**-yoo*

It hurts *(me)*
Doi-me
***doy**-muh*

Can you give me something
Pode-me dar alguma coisa para
***pod**-muh dar al**goo**muh **koy**-zuh pr*

I think I have an abscess
Creio que tenho um abcesso
***kray**oo kuh **ten**-yoo ooñ ab-**seh**-soo*

Can you repair my dentures?
Pode reparar a minha dentadura postiça?
*pod ruh-pa**rar** uh **meen**-yuh dentuh-**doo**ruh poosh-**tee**suh*

How much is it?
Quanto custa?
***kwan**too **koosh**tuh*

I need a receipt for my insurance
Preciso de um recibo para o seguro
*pre-**see**zoo dooñ ruh-**see**boo pro se**goo**roo*

■ **YOU MAY HEAR**

É preciso arrrancar
*e pre-**see**zoo aran**kar***
It has to come out

Vou-lhe dar uma injecção
vol**-yuh dar **oom**uh eenje**sowñ
I'm going to give you an injectio

...E	EM FRENTE	*ayñ frent*
...)	AO LADO DE	*ow **lah**-doo duh*
...)	PERTO DE	***pehr**too duh*
... LIGHTS	O SEMÁFORO	*oo suh-**ma**fooroo*
... CORNER	NA ESQUINA	*nuh **shkee**nuh*

...e me, sir / madam!
...favor, senhor / senhora!
*...r fa**vor** sun-**yor** / sun-**yor**uh*

How do I/we get to...?
Como se vai para...?
***koh**-moo suh vy **pa**ruh...*

...e station
...stação
*...ta**sowñ***

to the Gulbenkian
à Gulbenkian
*a gool-ben-**kyan***

to Rossio
ao Rossio
*ow roo**syoo***

...'re looking for...
...tamos à procura de...
*...ta-**moosh** a proo**koo**ruh duh...*

Is it far?
É longe?
e lonj

Can I walk there?
Pode-se ir a pé?
***pod**-suh eer uh pe*

...'re lost
...stamos perdidos
*...hta-**moosh** per**dee**-doosh*

Is this the right way to...?
É este o caminho para...?
*e aysht oo ka**meen**-yoo **pa**ruh...*

...ow do I/we get onto the motorway?
...Por onde se entra na auto-estrada?
*...poor **on**duh suh **ayn**truh nuh owtoo-**shtrah**-duh*

...an you show me where it is on the map?
Pode-me indicar onde está no mapa?
***pod**-muh eendee-**kar on**duh shta noo **mah**-puh*

■ YOU MAY HEAR

Depois de passar a ponte
*duh-**poysh** duh pa**sar** uh pont*
After passing the bridge

Volte à esquerda / direita
*volt a **shkehr**duh / dee**ray**-tuh*
Turn left / right

Siga sempre em frente até chegar a...
***see**-guh **sem**pruh ayñ frent a**te** shuh**gar** uh...*
Keep straight on until you get to...

■ BASICS ■ MAPS, GUIDES & NEWSPAPERS

What facilities do you have for disabled people?
Que instalações tem para deficientes?
*kuh eenshtaluh-**soynsh** tayñ **pa**ruh duh-feess-**yentsh***

Are there any toilets for the disabled?
Há casas de banho especiais para deficientes?
*a **kah**-zush duh **bahn**-yoo shpussee-**aysh** **pa**ruh duh-feess-**yentsh***

Do you have any bedrooms on the ground floor?
Tem alguns quartos no rés-do-chão?
*tayñ al**goonsh** **kwar**toosh noo resh-doo-**showñ***

Is there a lift?
Há elevador?
*a eeluh-vuh-**dor***

Where is the lift?
Onde é o elevador?
on**duh e oo eeluh-vuh-**dor

Are there any ramps?
Há rampas?
*a **ram**push*

Is there an induction loop?
Há auxiliares auditivos?
*a owseelee-**ah**-rush owdee-**tee**-voosh*

How many stairs are there?
Quantas escadas há?
***kwan**tush **shkah**-dush a*

How wide is the entrance door?
Qual é a largura da porta da entrada?
*kwal e uh lar**goo**-ruh duh **por**tuh dayn**trah**-duh*

Where is the wheelchair-accessible entrance?
Onde é o acesso para cadeiras de rodas?
***on**duh e oo a-**seh**-soo **pa**ruh ka**day**-rush duh **ro**dush*

Is there a reduction for handicapped people?
Há desconto para deficientes?
*a dush**kon**too **pa**ruh duh-feess-**yentsh***

Is there somewhere I can sit down?
Há algum sítio para me sentar?
*a al**gooñ** **seet**yoo **pa**ruh muh sen**tar***

■ ACCOMMODATION ■ HOTEL

HOSPITAL	HOSPITAL
BANCO (HOSPITAL)	CASUALTY DEPARTMENT
HORAS DE CONSULTA	SURGERY HOURS

I need a doctor
Preciso de um médico
*pre-**see**zoo dooñ **med**ikoo*

My son (daughter) is ill
O meu filho(a) está doente
*oo **may**oo **feel**-yoo(yuh) shta doo-**ent***

I'm diabetic
Sou diabético(a)
*soh dee-uh-**bet**ikoo(uh)*

I'm allergic to penicillin
Sou alérgico(a) a penicilina
*soh a**lehr**-jikoo(uh) uh punee-see**lee**nuh*

My blood group is...
O meu grupo sanguíneo é...
*oo **may**oo **groo**poo san**geen**-yoo e...*

Will he / she have to go to hospital?
Tem que ir para o hospital?
*tayñ kuh eer pro oshpee-**tal***

Will I have to pay?
Tenho que pagar?
ten**-yoo kuh pa**gar

I need a receipt for the insurance
Preciso de um recibo para o seguro
*pre-**see**zoo dooñ ruh-**see**boo pro se**goo**roo*

I have a pain here *(point)*
Doi-me aqui
doy**-muh a**kee

(s)he has a temperature
ele(a) tem febre
*ayl(uh) tayñ **feb**ruh*

I'm pregnant
Estou grávida
*shtoh **grav**iduh*

I'm on the pill
Tomo a pílula
***tom**oo uh **peel**oo-luh*

How much will it be?
Quanto será?
kwan**too suh-**rah

■ YOU MAY HEAR

Tem que entrar no hospital
*tayñ kuh ayn**trar** noo oshpee-**tal***
You will have to be admitted to hospital

Não é grave
nowñ e grav
It's not serious

■ BODY ■ EMERGENCIES ■ PHARMACY

If you want a small, strong black coffee ask for **um café** *(also known as* **uma bica***). A small, white coffee is* **um garoto***. An ordinary white coffee is* **um café com leite***. A large (mug-sized) coffee is* **um galão** *served in a tall glass. Tea is normally served in a teapot, weak and without any milk.*

a coffee
um café
*ooñ kuh-**fe***

a large milky coffee
um galão
*ooñ ga**lowñ***

a lager
uma cerveja
***oom**uh ser**vay**-juh*

a (strong) tea...
um chá (forte)...
ooñ sha (fort)...

with milk / lemon
com leite / limão
*koñ layt / lee**mowñ***

with toast
com torradas
*koñ too**rah**-dush*

for two
para dois
***pa**ruh doysh*

for me
para mim
***pa**ruh meeñ*

for him / her
para ele / ela
***pa**ruh ayl / eluh*

for us
para nós
***pa**ruh nosh*

with ice, please
com gelo, por favor
*koñ **jay**-loo poor fa**vor***

very hot, please
muito quente, por favor
mween**too kent poor fa**vor

a bottle of mineral water
uma garrafa de água mineral
oom**uh gar**rah**-fuh **dahg**-wuh meenuh-**ral

sparkling
com gás
koñ gas

still
sem gás
sayñ gas

Would you like a drink?
Quer uma bebida?
*kehr **oom**uh buh-**bee**duh*

What will you have?
Que quer tomar?
*kuh kehr too**mar***

I'm very thirsty
Tenho muita sede
***ten**-yoo **mween**tuh sed*

It's my round
É a minha vez
*e uh **meen**-yuh vesh*

■ OTHER DRINKS TO TRY

um chocolate *a chocolate, served hot* **quente** *or cold* **frio**
um chá de limão *boiling water poured over fresh lemon peel. A refreshing drink after a meal or at any time*
um batido de fruta *fruit milkshake: try strawberry –* **morango**

■ EATING OUT ■ WINES & SPIRITS

In Portugal lunch at restaurants is usually between 1230 and 1400. Dinner starts at 1900 or 1930 and goes on until 2130 or 2200. Café-type places serve meals any time. For those who prefer vegetarian dishes, turn to the VEGETARIAN topic for more prhases.

Where can I/we have a snack?
Onde se pode comer alguma coisa?
onduh suh pod koomehr algoomuh koy-zuh

not too expensive
não muito cara
nowñ mweentoo kah-ruh

Can you recommend a good local restaurant?
Pode recomendar um bom restaurante local?
pod ruh-koomendar ooñ boñ rushtoh-rant lookal

I'd like to book a table for ... people
Queria reservar uma mesa para ... pessoas
kree-uh ruh-zervar oomuh may-zuh paruh ... puh-so-ush

for tonight...
para esta noite...
paruh eshtuh noyt...

for tomorrow night...
para amanhã à noite...
paruh aman-yañ a noyt...

at 8pm
às 8 horas
ash oytoo orush

The menu, please
A ementa, por favor
uh eementuh poor favor

What is the dish of the day?
Qual é o prato do dia?
kwal e oo prah-too doo dee-uh

Do you have a set-price menu?
Tem a ementa do dia?
tayñ a eementuh doo dee-uh

I'll have this
Quero isto
kehroo eeshtoo

Can you recommend a local dish?
Pode recomendar uma especialidade local?
pod ruh-koomendar oomuh shpuss-yalee-dahd lookal

Excuse me!
Faz favor!
fash favor

Please bring...
Traga...
trah-guh...

more bread
mais pão
mysh powñ

more water
mais água
mysh ahg-wuh

more butter
mais manteiga
mysh mantay-guh

a half portion
meia dose
mayuh doh-zuh

another bottle
outra garrafa
oh-truh garrah-fuh

the bill
a conta
a kontuh

Is service included?
O serviço está incluido?
oo serveesoo shta een-klweedoo

EATING PLACES

Bar *serves drinks, coffee, snacks. Look out for:*
- ***pastéis de bacalhau*** *cod cakes*
- ***rissóis de camarão*** *prawn rissoles*
- ***um prego*** *a steak roll*

Café *and* **Cafetaria** *a cross between a bar and patissserie, with all sorts or hot or cold drinks and cakes as well as light meals. You can try:*
- ***uma sopa*** *soup, normally very tasty and cheap*
- ***um prego no prato*** *a small steak served generally with a fried egg and some chips*

Casa de Chá *an elegant patisserie which serves a variety of drinks despite its name (Tea House). Look out for:*
- ***bolos*** *a mouth-watering assortment of Portuguese cakes*
- ***torradas*** *toast*
- ***sandes*** *sandwiches – made with white bread and often cheese* ***queijo*** *; ham* ***fiambre*** *; or cured ham* ***presunto***

Casa de Pasto *simple, old-fashioned, cheap restaurant which usually offers good value meals at lunchtime*

Cervejaria *beer house, serving good lager and savouries, but generally offers a good menu, often specializing in seafood*

Churrascaria *restaurant serving barbecued food*

Esplanada *open-air café or restaurant*

Marisqueira *serves seafood as well as just drinks*

Pastelaria *patisserie or cake shop. A popular place for snacks at any time. Besides cakes and hot and cold drinks, it serves:*
- ***empadas*** *small chicken or veal pies*
- ***folhados de carne*** *meat pastries*
- ***croissants recheados*** *filled croissants*
- ***tostas*** *toasted sandwiches*

They will also serve soups for lunch and light meals. Cakes are, however, omnipresent, and are an immense attraction to sweet-toothed people

Restaurante *restaurant*

Tasca *or* **Tasquinha** *a small local tavern which were once cheap eating places but are becoming gentrified*

CONT...

■ ACEPIPES/SALGADOS APPETIZERS/SNACKS

azeitonas *olives*
camarões *shrimps*
chouriço *spicy red smoked sausage*
croquetes *croquettes (meat)*
febras *thin slices of roast pork*
gambas *prawns*
merendinha *oblong pastry filled with* **chouriço** *or ham*
panados *slices of meat in egg and breadcrumbs, fried*
pastéis de bacalhau *salt cod cakes (egg shaped)*
prego *steak roll*
prego no prato *small steak with fried egg and chips*
presunto *cured ham*
rissóis de camarão/peixe *shrimp or fish rissoles*
salpicão *slices of large* **chouriço**
sandes *sandwiches*
tosta *toasted sandwich*

■ ENTRADAS STARTER/FIRST COURSE

amêjoas à Bulhão Pato *clams with garlic and coriander*
espadarte fumado *smoked swordfish*
melão com presunto *slices of melon and cured ham*
salada de feijão frade *black-eyed bean salad dressed with olive oil, parsley, onion and slices of boiled egg*
santola/sapateira *spider crab/crab*

SOPAS SOUPS

caldo verde *green broth made with shredded kale and potato served with* **chouriço** *and maize bread*
canja *chicken soup*
sopa de coentros, alentejana *bread and coriander soup with a poached egg, Alentejo-style (a meal in itself)*
sopa de feijão *bean purée and vegetables*
sopa de legumes *vegetable purée*
sopa de marisco/peixe *shellfish/fish soup*

PRATOS DE CARNE — MEAT DISHES

bife *steak (and chips)*
bife à café *large steak in cream sauce (with chips)*
bife com ovo a cavalo *steak with fried egg on top (and chips)*
bife do lombo *sirloin steak*
bifes de perú *turkey steaks*
borrego (or anho) *spring lamb*
cabrito *kid*
caça (perdiz, codorniz, lebre) *game (partridge, quail, hare)*
carne de vaca *beef*
carneiro *mutton*
chanfana da Bairrada *kid stew*
coelho à caçadora *rabbit cooked in wine and herbs*
costeletas de porco *pork chops*
cozido à portuguesa *typical dish with boiled meats, sausages and vegetables*
entrecosto *entrecôte steak*
feijoada à Portuguesa *bean stew with pork meat and sausages*
fígado *liver*
frango na púcara/assado/de churrasco *chicken jugged/roasted/barbecued with hot sauce*
galinha *chicken*
iscas *typical dish of liver cooked in wine and garlic*
leitão à Bairrada *suckling pig crisply roasted*
lombinho de porco *pork loin*
pato assado com arroz *roast duck served with rice*
perú *turkey*
porco assado *roast pork*
porco à alentejana *typical dish with pork, clams and herbs*
rins com vinho do Porto *kidneys in port wine sauce*
rojões *crisp pieces of pork*
tripas à moda do Porto *tripe stew with beans and various meats*

CONT...

■ PEIXE E MARISCO **FISH AND SHELLFISH**

açorda de camarão *bread porridge with shrimps (or prawns)*
açorda de marisco *bread porridge with seafood*
amêijoas na cataplana *clams cooked in a sealed pot with spicy sausages and herbs*
arroz de lampreia/marisco/polvo *lamprey/seafood/octopus rice*
atum *tuna fish*
bacalhau à Brás *small strips of salt cod with egg and fried potatoes*
bacalhau à Gomes de Sá *salt cod in layers with potatoes and boiled eggs*
bacalhau com grão (Meia-Desfeita) *salt cod with chickpeas*
bacalhau na brasa *salt cod grilled on charcoal*
bifes de atum *tuna steaks*
caldeirada de enguias *eel stew*
caldeirada à Fragateira *rich fish stew with variety of fish*
carapaus (Joaquinzinhos) fritos *very small horse mackerel crisply fried (like whitebait)*
chocos com tinta *cuttlefish cooked in its own ink*
congro (or safio) *conger eel*
dourada *sea bream*
enguias fritas *fried eels*
espadarte *swordfish*
fataça *grey mullet*
filetes de pescada *hake fillets in batter*
gambas *prawns*
garoupa *grouper*
lagosta *lobster*
lagostins *king prawns*
linguado frito/grelhado *fried/grilled sole*
lulas à Algarvia/guisadas/recheadas *squid in garlic sauce/stewed/stuffed*

mexilhões *mussels*
ostras *oysters*
peixe espada frito/grelhado *fried/grilled scabbard fish*
pescada com todos *poached hake with boiled potatoes and vegetables*
pregado *turbot*
polvo *octopus*
robalo *sea bass*
salmonetes grelhados *grilled red mullet in butter and lemon*
sardinhas assadas *charcoal grilled sardines served with boiled potatoes, grilled peppers and salad*
sável *shad*
solha *plaice*
tamboril *monkfish*
truta grelhada *grilled trout*
salmão *salmon*

■ OVOS, LEGUMES, ACOMPANHAMENTOS
EGGS, VEGETABLES, SIDE DISHES

açorda de alho *bread porridge with garlic and beaten egg (normally served with fried fish)*
arroz branco *plain rice*
arroz de tomate *rice with tomato and onion*
arroz no forno *rice cooked in the oven*
batatas cozidas *boiled potatoes*
batadas assadas/fritas *baked potatoes/chips*
cenouras *carrots*
ervilhas *peas*
esparregado *green mousse (with spinach or turnip tops)*
espinafres *spinach*
favas *broad beans*
feijão verde cozido *french beans (boiled)*
ovos cozidos/estrelados *boiled/fried eggs*
ovos mexidos *scrambled eggs*

CONT...

omeleta simples *plain omelette:* ***de cogumelos*** *(mushroom),* ***de fiambre*** *(ham),* ***de queijo*** *(cheese)*
peixinhos da horta *french beans fried in batter*
puré de batata *mashed potato*
saladas *salads:* ***alface*** *(lettuce),* ***mista*** *(mixed),* ***tomate*** *(tomato),* ***pimentos assados*** *(grilled peppers)*
Russian salad *mixed cooked vegetables with mayonnaise*

■ USEFUL COOKERY TERMS

albardado	**in batter**
assado	**baked/roasted**
assado no espeto	**spit roasted**
bem passado	**well done** *(meat)*
caldeirada	**fish stew**
churrasco	**barbecued/cooked on charcoal**
cozido	**boiled/poached**
ensopado	**stew served on slices of bread**
espetada	**kebab**
estufado	**braised**
fumado	**smoked**
frito	**fried**
grelhado	**grilled**
guisado	**stewed**
mal passado	**rare** *(meat)*
molho	**sauce**
na brasa	**on charcoal**
no forno	**in the oven**
recheado	**stuffed/filled with...**
salteado	**sautéed**

■ SOBREMESAS — DESSERTS

What desserts are there?
Que sobremesas tem?
*kuh sobruh-**may**-zush tayñ*

arroz doce *rice pudding Portuguese-style*
fruta da época *fruit in season*
gelado *ice cream*
laranja descascada *finely-sliced, fresh, peeled orange sprinkled with sugar*
leite-creme *crème brûlée*
maçã assada *large baked russet apple*
pudim da casa *restaurant's own speciality*
pudim de coco *coconut pudding*
pudim flan *crème caramel*
pudim Molotov *egg-white pudding covered with egg sauce*
salada de fruta *fruit salad*
tarte de amêndoa *almond tart*
torta de laranja *rolled-up orange and egg pudding*
toucinho do céu *literally 'bacon from heaven', an egg and almond pudding*

■ QUEIJOS — CHEESES

What cheeses do you have?
Que queijos tem?
kuh ***kay****-joosh tayñ*

queijo fresco *fresh cheese (can be large or small)*
queijo da Ilha *literally 'cheese from the Island': a hard strong cheddar-type cheese from the Azores*
queijo da Serra/amanteigado *cheese from the mountain/ buttery – the king of cheeses in Portugal. A soft, runny cheese that can be eaten with a spoon. It comes from the Serra da Estrela and is made with ewe's milk*
queijos de ovelha *small, slightly cured, ewe's milk cheeses from Azeitão and Évora*
queijinhos secos *small well-cured cheeses made from ewe's or goat's milk (or both), produced countrywide*
requeijão *fresh curd cheese resembling ricotta*

■ DRINKING ■ VEGETARIAN ■ WINES & SPIRITS

POLÍCIA	POLICE
AMBULÂNCIA	AMBULANCE
BOMBEIROS	FIRE BRIGADE
BANCO DO HOSPITAL	CASUALTY DEPARTMENT

Help!
Socorro!
*soo**korr**oo*

Fire!
Fogo!
***foh**-goo*

Can you help me?
Pode-me ajudar?
pod**-muh ajoo**dar

There's been an accident!
Houve um acidente!
*ohv ooñ asee**dent***

Someone is injured
Há um ferido
*a ooñ fe**ree**doo*

Someone has been knocked down by a car
Alguém foi atropelado
*al**gayñ** foy atroopuh-**lad**oo*

Call...
Chame...
sham...

the police
a polícia
*uh poo**leess**-yuh*

an ambulance
uma ambulância
***oom**uh amboo**lanss**-yuh*

please
por favor
*poor fa**vor***

Where's the police station?
Onde é a esquadra?
***on**duh e uh **shkwah**-druh*

I want to report a theft
Quero participar um roubo
***kehr**oo purteesee**par** ooñ **roh**-boo*

I've been robbed
Fui roubado(a)
*fwee roh-**bah**-doo(uh)*

I've been attacked
Fui agredido(a)
*fwee agruh-**dee**-doo(uh)*

Someone's stolen my...
Roubaram-me...
*roh-**bah**-rowñ-muh...*

bag
a mala
*uh **mah**-luh*

passport
o passaporte
*oo passuh-**port***

traveller's cheques
os cheques de viagem
*oosh sheksh duh vee-**ah**-jayñ*

money
o dinheiro
*oo deen-**yay**-roo*

My car's been broken into
Assaltaram-me o carro
*assal-**tah**-rowñ-muh oo **karr**oo*

My car's been stolen
Roubaram-me o carro
*roh-**bah**-rowñ-muh oo **karr**oo*

I've been raped
Violaram-me
*vyo**lah**-rowñ-muh*

I am lost
Perdi-me
*per**dee**-muh*

I want to speak to a policewoman
Quero falar com uma mulher-polícia
***keh**roo fa**lar** koñ **oom**uh mool-**yehr** poo**leess**-yuh*

I need to make an urgent telephone call
Preciso de fazer uma chamada urgente
*pre-**see**zoo duh fa**zehr** **oom**uh sha**mah**-duh oor**jent***

I need a report for my insurance
Preciso de um relatório para o meu seguro
*pre-**see**zoo dooñ rela**tor**yoo pro **may**oo se**goo**roo*

I didn't know the speed limit
Não sabia qual era o limite de velocidade
*nowñ sa**bee**-uh kwal **e**ruh oo lee**meet** duh vuh-loossee-**dahd***

How much is the fine?
Quanto é a multa?
***kwan**too e uh **mool**ta*

Where do I pay?
Onde pago?
***on**duh **pah**goo*

Do I have to pay straightaway?
Tenho que pagar já?
***ten**-yoo kuh pa**gar** jah*

I'm very sorry
Lamento muito
*la**men**too **mween**too*

■ YOU MAY HEAR

Posso ajudar?
poss**oo ajoo**dar
Can I help you?

Passou a luz vermelha
*pa**ssoh** uh loosh ver**mel**-yuh*
You went through a red light

■ BODY ■ DOCTOR

In cities Tourist Offices will give you What's On, a magazine listing events and entertainment. Newspapers carry pages advertising local events.

What is there to do in the evenings?
Que se pode fazer à noite?
*kuh suh pod fa**zehr** a noyt*

Do you know what events are on this week?
Sabe que actividades culturais há esta semana?
*sab kuh ateevee-**dah**-dush kool-too-**rysh** a **esh**tuh se**mah**-nuh*

Is there anything for children?
Há alguma coisa para crianças?
*a al**goo**muh **koy**-zuh **pa**ruh kree-**an**sush*

Where can I/we get tickets...?
Onde se arranjam bilhetes de...?
***on**duh see arran**jowñ** beel-**yetsh**...*

for tonight
para esta noite
*pra **esh**tuh noyt*

for the show
para o espectáculo
*pro shpe-**tak**ooloo*

for the football match
para o jogo de futebol
*pro **joh**-goo duh foot**bol***

I'd like ... tickets
Queria ... bilhetes
kree**-uh ... beel-**yetsh

...adults
...para adultos
*...pra **dool**toosh*

...children
...para crianças
*...pra kree-**an**sush*

Where can we go dancing?
Onde se pode dançar?
on**duh suh pod dan**sar

What time does it open?
A que horas abre?
*uh kee **o**ruz **ah**-bruh*

How much is it to get in?
Quanto é a entrada?
***kwan**too e uh ayn**trah**-duh*

Is there a casino?
Há um casino?
*a ooñ ka**zee**-noo*

■ YOU MAY HEAR

A entrada custa ... escudos com direito a consumo
*uh ayn**trah**-duh **koosh**tuh...**shkoo**doosh koñ dee-**ray**too uh kon**soo**moo*
It costs ... escudos to get in including a free drink

■ CINEMA ■ SIGHTSEEING & TOURIST OFFICE ■ THEATRE

*To fax Portugal from the UK, the code is **00 351** followed by the Portuguese area code, e.g. Lisbon **1**, Oporto **2**, and then the fax number you require.*

ADDRESSING A FAX	
FROM	DE
FOR THE ATTENTION OF	À ATENÇÃO DE
DATE	DATA
RE:	REF.
THIS DOCUMENT CONTAINS ...	ESTE DOCUMENTO CONTEM ...
PAGES INCLUDING THIS	PÁGINAS, INCLUINDO ESTA

Do you have a fax?
Tem fax?
tayñ fax

I want to send a fax
Queria mandar um fax
***kree**-uh man**dar** ooñ fax*

What is your fax number?
Qual é o seu número de fax?
*kwal e oo **say**oo **noo**meroo duh fax*

I am having trouble getting through to your fax
Não consigo mandar-lhe o fax
*nowñ kon**see**goo man**dar**-lyuh oo fax*

Please resend your fax
Por favor repita o fax
*poor fa**vor** ruh**pee**tuh oo fax*

I can't read it
Não o posso ler
*nowñ oo **pos**soo lehr*

The fax is constantly engaged
O fax está constantemente impedido
*oo fax shta konshtant-**ment** eempuh-**dee**doo*

Can I send a fax from here?
Posso mandar um fax daqui?
pos**soo man**dar** ooñ fax duh**kee

■ LETTERS ■ TELEPHONE

beef	**a carne de vaca**	*karn duh **vah**-kuh*
biscuits	**as bolachas**	*bool**ah**-shush*
bread	**o pão**	*powñ*
bread *(brown)*	**o pão integral**	*powñ eentuh-**gral***
bread roll	**o papo-seco**	***pah**poo-**seh**-koo*
butter	**a manteiga**	*man**tay**-guh*
cakes	**os bolos**	***boh**-loosh*
cheese	**o queijo**	***kay**-joo*
chicken	**a galinha**	*ga**leen**-yuh*
coffee	**o café**	*kuh-**fe***
cream	**a nata**	***nah**-tuh*
crisps	**as batatas fritas**	*ba**tah**-tush **free**tush*
eggs	**os ovos**	***oh**-voosh*
fish	**o peixe**	*paysh*
flour	**a farinha**	*fa**reen**-yuh*
ham *(cooked)*	**o fiambre**	*fee-**am**-bruh*
ham *(cured)*	**o presunto**	*pruh-**zoon**too*
honey	**o mel**	*mel*
jam	**a compota**	*kom**pot**uh*
lamb	**o carneiro**	*kar**nay**-roo*
margarine	**a margarina**	*marguh-**ree**nuh*
marmalade	**a doce de laranja**	*dohss duh la**ran**juh*
milk	**o leite**	*layt*
olive oil	**o azeite**	*a**zayt***
orange juice	**o sumo de laranja**	***soo**moo duh la**ran**juh*
pasta	**as massas**	***mass**ush*
pepper	**a pimenta**	*pee**men**tuh*
pork	**a carne de porco**	*karn duh **por**koo*
rice	**o arroz**	*ar**osh***
salt	**o sal**	*sal*
stock cube	**o cubo concentrado**	***koo**boo kon-sayn**trah**-doo*
sugar	**o açúcar**	*a**soo**kar*
tea	**o chá**	*sha*
tin of tomatoes	**a lata de tomates**	***lah**tuh duh to-**matsh***
vinegar	**o vinagre**	*vee**nah**-gruh*

apples	**as maçãs**	*ma**sañsh***
apricots	**os damascos**	*da**mash**koosh*
asparagus	**os espargos**	***shpar**goosh*
aubergine	**a beringela**	*bereen-**je**luh*
bananas	**as bananas**	*ba**nah**-nush*
cabbage	**a couve**	*kohv*
carrots	**as cenouras**	*suh-**noh**-rush*
cauliflower	**a couve-flor**	*kohv-**flor***
cherries	**as cerejas**	*suh-**ray**-jush*
courgettes	**as courgettes**	*koor**jetsh***
french beans	**o feijão verde**	*fay-jowñ-**vehrd***
garlic	**o alho**	***al**-yoo*
grapefruit	**a toranja**	*too**ran**-juh*
grapes	**as uvas**	***oo**vush*
leeks	**os alhos-porros**	*al-yoosh-**por**rosh*
lemon	**o limão**	*lee**mowñ***
lettuce	**a alface**	*al**fass***
melon	**o melão**	*me**lowñ***
mushrooms	**os cogumelos**	*koogoo-**me**loosh*
nectarines	**as nectarinas**	*nek-tuh-**ree**nush*
onions	**as cebolas**	*suh-**bo**lush*
oranges	**as laranjas**	*la**ran**jush*
peaches	**os pêssegos**	***peh**-suh-goosh*
pears	**as pêras**	***peh**-rush*
peas	**as ervilhas**	*ehr**veel**-yush*
peppers	**os pimentos**	*pee**men**toosh*
pineapple	**o ananás**	*anuh-**nash***
plums	**as ameixas**	*a**may**-shush*
potatoes	**as batatas**	*ba**tah**-tush*
raspberries	**as framboesas**	*fram-**bway**-zush*
spinach	**os espinafres**	*shpee-**na**frush*
strawberries	**os morangos**	*moo**ran**goosh*
tomatoes	**os tomates**	*too**matsh***
turnips	**os nabos**	***nah**-boosh*
watermelon	**a melancia**	*melan-**see**-uh*

Frequent greetings include **olá, como está** *and* **bom dia Senhor...** *or* **Senhora...** *. If you are saying good night and leaving you would say* **adeus, boa noite** *.*

Hello!
Olá!
*oh-**la***

Goodbye!
Adeus!
*a**day**-oosh*

Good morning *(until noon)*
Bom dia
*boñ **dee**-uh*

Good afternoon *(from noon until dusk)*
Boa tarde
***boh**-uh tard*

Good evening / Good night *(after dark)*
Boa noite
***boh**-uh noyt*

Pleased to meet you
Muito prazer
ween**too pra**zehr

It's a pleasure
É um prazer
*e ooñ pra**zehr***

How are you?
Como está?
***koh**-moo shta*

Fine, thanks
Bem, obrigado(a)
*bayñ oh-bree**gah**-doo(uh)*

And you?
E você?
*ee voh-**se***

How are things?
Como vai?
***koh**-moo vy*

See you tomorrow
Até amanhã
*a**te** aman-**yañ***

See you later
Até logo
*a**te** **log**oo*

Until we meet again
Até à vista
*a**te** a **veesh**-tuh*

These phrases are intended for use at the hotel desk. More details about rooms can be found in the ACCOMMODATION topic.

Do you have a room for tonight?
Tem um quarto para esta noite?
*tayñ ooñ **kwar**too **pa**ruh **esh**tuh noyt*

I booked a room...
Reservei um quarto...
*ruh-zer**vay** ooñ **kwar**too...*

in the name of...
em nome de...
ayñ nom duh...

I'd like to see the room
Queria ver o quarto
***kree**-uh vehr oo **kwar**too*

Have you anything else?
Tem outra coisa?
*tayñ **oh**-truh **koy**-zuh*

Where can I park the car?
Onde posso estacionar o carro?
***on**duh **poss**oo shtass-yoo**nar** oo **karr**oo*

What time is...?
A que hora é...?
*uh kee **or**uh e...*

dinner
o jantar
*oo jan**tar***

breakfast
o pequeno-almoço
*oo puh-**kay**noo al**moh**-soo*

We'll be back late tonight
Esta noite voltamos tarde
***esh**tuh noyt vol**tuh**-moosh tard*

Do you lock the door?
Fecham a porta?
*fay-**showñ** uh **por**tuh*

The key for room number...
A chave do quarto número...
*uh shahv doo **kwar**too **noo**meroo...*

Are there any messages for me?
Há algumas mensagens para mim?
*a al**goo**mush men**sah**-jayñsh **pa**ruh meeñ*

I'm leaving tomorrow
Vou-me embora amanhã
voh**-muh em**boh**-ruh aman-**yañ

Please prepare the bill
Por favor faça a conta
*poor fa**vor** **fah**-sa **kon**tuh*

Can I leave my luggage until...?
Posso deixar a minha bagagem até...?
***poss**oo **day**shar uh **meen**-yuh ba**gah**-jayñ a**te**...*

■ ACCOMMODATION ■ ROOM SERVICE

The Single European Market allows goods within the EU to travel freely. Businesses which supply goods to VAT-registered EU companies are required to complete a Sales List which accompanies the goods. The Portuguese VAT registration code (IVA – **Imposto de Valor Acrescentado***) consists of a 9-digit number. This code is called* **Número de Contribuinte** *(number of contributor – tax payer).*

What is your fiscal code number *(IVA number)***?**
Qual é o seu número de contribuinte?
*kwal e oo **say**oo **noo**meroo duh kontree**bween**tuh*

Our VAT number is... *(**GB** followed by number)*
O nosso número IVA é...
*oo **noss**oo **noo**meroo **ee**vuh e...*

The goods should be delivered to...
A mercadoria deve ser entregue a...*(person)* **/ em...** *(place)*
*uh merkadoo-**ree**-uh dev sehr ayn**treh**-guh... / ayñ...*

The consignment must be accompanied by a pro forma invoice
A remessa deve ser acompanhada de uma factura pró-forma
*uh ruh**mess**uh dev sehr akompan-**ya**-duh **doo**muh fak**too**ruh pro**for**muh*

How long will it take to deliver?
Qual será o prazo de entrega?
*kwal suh-**rah** oo **prah**-zoo dayn**treh**-guh*

Delivery will take ... days / weeks
A entrega será feita dentro de ... dias / semanas
*uh ayn**treh**-guh suh-**rah** **fay**tuh **den**troo duh ... **dee**-ush / se**mah**-nush*

Please confirm safe delivery of the goods
Por favor confirme se a entrega foi feita em boas condições
*poor fa**vor** kom**feer**-muh see uh ayn**treh**-guh foy **fay**-tuh ayñ **boh**-ush kondee-**soynsh***

Is it necessary to insure the goods?
É necessário fazer seguro da mercadoria?
*e nussuh-**sar**-yoo fa**zehr** se**goo**roo duh merkadoo-**ree**-uh*

■ NUMBERS ■ OFFICE

DRY-CLEANER'S	A TINTURARIA / A LIMPEZA A SECO
LAUNDERETTE	A LAVANDARIA AUTOMÁTICA
WASHING POWDER	O DETERGENTE EM PÓ

Where can I do some washing?
Onde posso lavar alguma roupa?
__on__duh __poss__oo la__var__ al__goo__muh __roh__-puh

Do you have a laundry service?
Tem serviço de lavandaria?
tayñ ser__vee__soo duh lavanduh-__ree__-uh

When will my things be ready?
Quando estão prontas as minhas coisas?
__kwan__doo shtowñ __pron__tush ush __meen__-yush __koy__-zush

Is there a launderette near here?
Há uma lavandaria automática perto daqui?
a __oo__muh lavanduh-__ree__-uh owtoo__ma__tikuh __pehr__too duh__kee__

When does it open?
Quando abre?
__kwan__doo __ah__-bruh

When does it close?
Quando fecha?
__kwan__doo __fay__shuh

Does it work with coins?
Trabalha com moedas?
tra__bal__-yuh koñ __mway__-dush

Which?
Quais?
kwaysh

Where can I dry some clothes?
Onde posso secar alguma roupa?
__on__duh __poss__oo se__kar__ al__goo__muh __roh__-puh

Can you iron these clothes?
Pode passar esta roupa a ferro?
pod pa__sar__ __esh__tuh __roh__-puh uh __fer__roo

Can I borrow an iron?
Pode-me emprestar um ferro de engomar?
__pod__-muh aympresh-__tar__ ooñ __fer__roo duh ayngoo-__mar__

■ ROOM SERVICE

Where can I/we go...?
Onde se pode...?
***on**duh suh pod...*

fishing
pescar
*push**kar***

riding
andar a cavalo
*an**dar** uh ka**vah**-loo*

play golf
jogar golfe
*joo**gar** golf*

play tennis
jogar ténis
*joo**gar tay**-neesh*

Are there any good beaches near here?
Há algumas praias boas aqui perto?
*a al**goo**mush **pry**-ush **boh**-ush a**kee pehr**too*

Is there a swimming pool?
Há piscina?
*a peesh-**see**nuh*

Where can I/we hire bikes?
Onde se pode alugar bicicletas?
***on**duh suh pod aloo**gar** beesee-**kle**tush*

Do you have helmets?
Tem capacetes?
*tayñ kapuh-**setsh***

How much is it...?
Quanto é...?
***kwan**too e...*

per hour
por hora
*poor **or**uh*

per day
por dia
*poor **dee**-uh*

What do you do in your spare time? *(familiar)*
Que fazes nas horas livres?
*kuh **fah**-zush nuz **or**ush **lee**vrush*

I like...
Eu gosto de...
***ay**-oo **gosh**too duh...*

painting
pintar
*peen**tar***

sunbathing
tomar banhos de sol
*too**mar bahn**-yoosh duh sol*

Do you like...? *(formal)*
Gosta de...?
***gosh**tuh duh...*

Do you like...? *(familiar)*
Gostas...?
***gosh**tush...*

■ CINEMA ■ MUSIC ■ SPORTS ■ TELEVISION ■ THEATRE

17 May 1994	17 de Maio de 1995
Dear Sirs	Caros Senhores *(commercial letter)*
Dear Sir / Madam	Caro Senhor / Cara Senhora
Yours faithfully	Atentamente
Dear Mr... / Dear Mrs...	Estimado Sr.... / Estimada Sra....
Yours sincerely	Com muitos cumprimentos
Dear Paula	Querida Paula
Best regards	Um abraço
Dear Carlos	Querido Carlos
Love	Um grande abraço *or* Beijos

Further to your letter of 7 May...
Com referência à sua carta de 7 de Maio...

Further to our telephone conversation...
Com referência à nossa conversa telefónica...

I enclose... / We enclose
Junto... / Juntamos...

Thank you for the information / your price list
Agradeço a sua informação / a sua lista de preços

We are very sorry, but we are unable to...
Lamentamos muito não poder...

I look forward to hearing from you
Aguardando as suas notícias

by return [of] post
pela volta do correio

■ **FAX** ■ **OFFICE**

BAGGAGE RECLAIM	A RECOLHA DE BAGAGEM
LEFT LUGGAGE OFFICE	O DEPÓSITO DE BAGAGENS
TROLLEY	O CARRINHO

My luggage hasn't arrived
A minha bagagem não chegou
*uh **meen**-yuh ba**gah**-jayñ nowñ shuh-**goh***

My suitcase has arrived damaged
A minha mala chegou danificada
*uh **meen**-yuh **mah**-luh shuh-**goh** duhneefee-**kah**-duh*

What's happened to the luggage on the flight from...?
Que se passa com a bagagem do voo de...?
*kuh suh **pass**uh koñ uh ba**gah**-jayñ doo **voh**-oo duh...*

Can you help me with my luggage, please?
Pode-me ajudar com a bagagem, por favor?
pod**-muh ajoo**dar** koñ uh ba**gah**-jayñ poor fa**vor

When does the left luggage office open / close?
Quando abre / fecha o depósito de bagagens?
***kwan**doo **ah**-bruh / **fay**shuh oo duh-**poz**itoo duh ba**gah**-jaynsh*

I'd like to leave this suitcase...
Queria deixar esta mala...
***kree**-uh day**shar** **esh**tuh **mah**-luh...*

until ... o'clock
até ... horas
*a**te** ... **or**ush*

overnight
durante a noite
*doo**rant** uh noyt*

till Saturday
até sábado
*a**te** **sa**badoo*

I'll collect it at...
Venho buscá-la às...
***ven**-yoo boosh-**ka**-luh ash...*

Can I leave my luggage?
Posso deixar a minha bagagem?
***poss**oo day**shar** uh **meen**-yuh ba**gah**-jayñ*

■ YOU MAY HEAR

Pode deixá-la aqui até às seis
*pod day**sha**-luh a**kee** a**te** ash saysh*
You can leave it here until 6 o'clock

In this section we have used the familiar form ***tu*** *for the questions.* ***Tu*** *is widely used between young people soon after being introduced and between close friends and relatives – at any age.*

What's your name?
Como te chamas?
***koh**-moo tuh **shah**-mush*

My name is...
Chamo-me...
***shah**-moo-muh...*

How old are you?
Quantos anos tens?
***kwan**toosh **ah**-noosh tayñsh*

I'm ... years old
Tenho ... anos
***ten**-yoo ... **ah**-noosh*

Are you Portuguese?
És português(a)?
*es poortoo-**gesh**(uh)*

I'm English *(masc.)*
Sou inglês
*soh een**glesh***

I'm English *(fem.)*
Sou inglesa
*soh een**gle**zuh*

Where do you live?
Onde vives?
***on**duh **vee**vush*

Where do you live? *(plural)*
Onde vivem?
on**duh vee**vayñ

I live in London
Vivo em Londres
***vee**-voo ayñ **lon**drush*

We live in Glasgow
Vivemos em Glasgow
*vee-**veh**-moosh ayñ **glas**gow*

I'm still studying
Sou estudante
*soh shtoo**dant***

I work
Trabalho
*tra**bal**-yoo*

I'm retired
Sou reformado(a)
*soh refoor**mah**-doo(uh)*

I'm...
Sou...
soh...

single
solteiro(a)
*sol**tay**-roo(uh)*

married
casado(a)
*ka**zah**-doo(uh)*

divorced
divorciado(a)
*deevoors-**yah**-doo(uh)*

I have...
Tenho...
***ten**-yoo...*

a boyfriend
namorado
*namoo-**rah**-doo*

a girlfriend
namorada
*namoo-**rah**-duh*

a partner
companheiro(a)
*kompan-**yay**-roo(uh)*

I have ... children
Tenho ... filhos
***ten**-yoo ... **feel**-yoosh*

I have no children
Não tenho filhos
*nowñ **ten**-yoo **feel**-yoosh*

I'm here...
Estou aqui...
*shtoh a**kee**...*

on holiday
de férias
*duh **fehr**-yush*

for work
por motivo de trabalho
*poor moo**tee**-voo duh tra**bal**-yoo*

Have you...? Tem...? *tayñ...*

a map of *(name town)* um mapa de... *ooñ **mah**-puh duh...*

of the region da região *duh ruj-**yowñ***

Can you show me where ... is on the map?
Pode-me mostrar onde fica ... no mapa?
***pod**-muh moosh-**trar on**duh **fee**kuh ... noo **mah**-puh*

Do you have a detailed map of the area?
Tem um mapa detalhado da área?
*tayñ ooñ **mah**-puh duhtal-**yah**-doo duh **a**ree-uh*

Can you draw me a map?
Pode-me desenhar um mapa?
***pod**-muh duhsen-**yar** ooñ **mah**-puh*

Have you...? Tem...? *tayñ...*

a guide book algum guia *al**gooñ ghee**-uh*

a leaflet algum folheto *al**gooñ** fool-**yet**oo*

in English? em inglês? *ayñ een**glesh***

I'd like the English language version *(of a cassette guide)*
Gostaria da versão inglesa (da cassette)
*gooshtuh-**ree**-uh duh ver**sowñ** een**gle**zuh (duh ka**sset**)*

Where can I/we buy an English newspaper?
Onde se pode comprar um jornal inglês?
on**duh suh pod kom**prar** ooñ joor**nal** een**glesh

Do you have any English newspapers / novels?
Tem jornais / romances ingleses?
*tayñ joor**naysh** / roo**man**-sush een**gle**zush*

When do the English newspapers arrive?
Quando chegam os jornais ingleses?
***kwan**doo sheh**gowñ** oosh joor**naysh** een**gle**zush*

Please reserve *(name newspaper)* **for me**
Pode-me reservar o ... por favor
pod**-muh ruh-zer**var** oo ... poor fa**vor

■ DIRECTIONS ■ SIGHTSEEING & TOURIST OFFICE

LIQUIDS

1/2 litre... *(c.1 pint)*	**meio litro de...**	***may**oo **lee**troo duh...*
a litre of...	**um litro de...**	*ooñ **lee**troo duh...*
1/2 bottle of...	**meia garrafa de...**	***may**uh gar**rah**-fuh duh ...*
a bottle of...	**uma garrafa de...**	***oom**uh gar**rah**-fuh duh...*
a glass of...	**um copo de...**	*ooñ **kop**oo duh...*

WEIGHTS

100 grams of...	**cem gramas de...**	*sayñ **grah**-mush duh...*
1/2 kilo of... *(500g)*	**meio quilo de...**	***may**oo **kee**loo duh...*
1 kilo of...	**um quilo de...**	*ooñ **kee**loo duh...*

FOOD

a slice of...	**uma fatia de...**	***oom**uh fa**tee**-uh duh...*
a portion of...	**uma porção de...**	***oom**uh poor**sowñ** duh...*
a dozen...	**uma dúzia de...**	***oom**uh **doo**zee-uh duh...*
a box of...	**uma caixa de...**	***oom**uh **ky**-shuh duh...*
a packet of...	**um pacote de...**	*ooñ pa**kot** duh...*
a tin of...	**uma lata de...**	***oom**uh **lah**-tuh duh...*
a jar of...	**um boião de...**	*ooñ boy-**owñ** duh...*

MISCELLANEOUS

1000 escudos of...	**mil escudos de...**	*meel **shkoo**doosh duh...*
a half	**metade**	*muh-**tahd***
a quarter	**um quarto**	*ooñ **kwar**too*
ten per cent	**dez por cento**	*desh poor **sen**too*
more...	**mais...**	*mysh...*
less...	**menos...**	***meh**-noosh...*
enough	**chega**	***sheh**-guh*
double	**o dobro**	*oo **doh**-broo*
twice	**duas vezes**	***doo**-ush **veh**-zush*
three times	**três vezes**	*tresh **veh**-zush*

■ FOOD ■ SHOPPING

You can buy either ***uma caderneta de 10 viagens*** *, which is valid for 10 journeys (no date limit) or* ***um passe*** *, which covers a month's travel on both bus and metro.*

ENTRADA	**ENTRANCE**
SAÍDA	**WAY OUT / EXIT**
LINHA DE METRO	**METRO LINE**

Where is the nearest metro station?
Onde é a estação de metro mais próxima?
__on__duh e uh shta__sowñ__ duh __me__troo mysh __pross__imuh

How does the ticket machine work?
Como funciona a máquina automática?
__koh__-moo foonss-__yo__nuh uh __mak__inuh owtoo__ma__tikuh

Do you have a map of the metro?
Tem um mapa do metro?
tayñ ooñ __mah__-puh doo __me__troo

I'm going to...
Vou a...
voh uh...

How do I/we get to...?
Como se vai para...?
__koh__-moo suh vy __pa__ruh...

Do I have to change?
Tenho que mudar?
__ten__-yoo kuh moo__dar__

Which line is it for...?
Qual é a linha para...?
kwal e uh __leen__-yuh __pa__ruh...

In which direction?
Em que direcção?
ayñ kuh dee__reh__sowñ

What is the next stop?
Qual é a próxima paragem?
kwal e uh __pross__imuh pa__rah__-jayñ

Excuse me!
Por favor!
poor fa__vor__

Please let me through
Pode-me deixar passar?
__pod__-muh day__shar__ pa__ssar__

I'm getting off here
Desço aqui
__desh__-soo a__kee__

■ BUS ■ TAXI

Banks are generally open 0830-1500, Monday to Friday. Double-check opening hours when you arrive as these may be different in some towns.

CAIXA AUTOMÁTICA	CASH DISPENSER
INTRODUZA O SEU CARTÃO	INSERT YOUR CARD
MARQUE O SEU NÚMERO	ENTER YOUR PERSONAL NUMBER
LEVANTAMENTO	CASH WITHDRAWAL
RETIRE O CARTÃO	REMOVE YOUR CARD
OPERAÇÃO EM PROCESSO	WE ARE DEALING WITH YOUR REQUEST
AGUARDE POR FAVOR	PLEASE WAIT

Where can I/we change some money?
Onde se pode trocar dinheiro?
__on__duh suh pod troo__kar__ deen-__yay__-roo

I want to change these traveller's cheques
Quero trocar estes cheques de viagem
__keh__roo troo__kar__ __esh__tush sheksh duh vee-__ah__-jayñ

When does the bank open?
Quando abre o banco?
__kwan__doo __ah__-bruh oo __ban__koo

When does the bank close?
Quando fecha o banco?
__kwan__doo __fay__shuh oo __ban__koo

Can I pay with pounds / dollars?
Posso pagar em libras / dólares?
__poss__oo pa__gar__ ayñ __lee__brush / __do__larush

Can I use my credit card to get escudos?
Posso obter escudos com o meu cartão de crédito?
__poss__oo ob__tehr__ __shkoo__doosh koñ oo __may__oo kar__towñ__ duh __kred__itoo

Can I use my card with this cash dispenser?
Posso usar o meu cartão nesta Caixa?
__poss__oo oo__zar__ oo __may__oo kar__towñ__ __nesh__tuh __ky__-shuh

Do you have any loose change?
Tem trocos?
tayñ __tro__koosh

■ PAYING

Are there any good concerts on?
Há algum bom concerto por aqui?
*a al**goom** boñ kon**sehr**-too poor a**kee***

Where can one get tickets?
Onde se compram os bilhetes?
on**duh suh kom**prowñ** oosh beel-**yetsh

Where can we hear some fado / folklore?
Onde podemos ouvir o fado / folclore?
***on**duh poo**deh**-moosh oh-**veer** oo **fah**-doo / folk**lo**ruh*

What sort of music do you like?
De que música gosta?
*duh kuh **moo**zikuh **gosh**tuh*

I like...
Gosto de...
***gosh**too duh...*

Which is your favourite group?
Qual o seu conjunto preferido?
*kwal oo **say**oo kon**joon**-too pruhfuh-**ree**-doo*

Who is your favourite singer?
De que artista gosta mais?
*duh kuh ar**teesh**tuh **gosh**tuh mysh*

Can you play any musical instruments?
Sabe tocar algum instrumento musical?
*sab too**kar** al**gooñ** eenshtroo-**men**too moozi**kal***

I play...	**the guitar**	**the piano**	**the clarinet**
Toco...	a guitarra	o piano	o clarinete
***toh**-koo...*	*uh ghee**tah**-rruh*	*oo pee-**ah**-noo*	*oo klaree-**net***

Have you been to any good concerts recently?
Esteve em algum concerto bom ultimamente?
*shtehv ayñ al**gooñ** kon**sehr**-too boñ ooltimuh**ment***

Do you like opera?
Gosta de ópera?
***gosh**tuh **do**peruh*

Do you like pop music? *(familiar)*
Gostas de música pop?
***gosh**tush duh **moo**zikuh pop*

■ ENTERTAINMENT ■ MAKING FRIENDS

0	**zero**	***zehr**-oo*
1	**um (uma)**	*ooñ (**oom**uh)*
2	**dois (duas)**	*doysh (**doo**-uz)*
3	**três**	*tresh*
4	**quatro**	***kwa**troo*
5	**cinco**	***seen**koo*
6	**seis**	*saysh*
7	**sete**	*set*
8	**oito**	***oy**too*
9	**nove**	*nov*
10	**dez**	*desh*
11	**onze**	*onz*
12	**doze**	*dohz*
13	**treze**	*trezh*
14	**catorze**	*ka**torz***
15	**quinze**	*keenz*
16	**dezasseis**	*dezuh-**saysh***
17	**dezassete**	*dezuh-**set***
18	**dezoito**	*de**zoy**too*
19	**dezanove**	*dezuh-**nov***
20	**vinte**	*veent*
21	**vinte e um**	*veentee-**ooñ***
22	**vinte e dois**	*veentee-**doysh***
23	**vinte e três**	*veentee-**tresh***
24	**vinte e quatro**	*veentee-**kwa**troo*
25	**vinte e cinco**	*veentee-**seen**koo*
26	**vinte e seis**	*veentee-**saysh***
27	**vinte e sete**	*veentee-**set***
28	**vinte e oito**	*veentee-**oy**too*
29	**vinte e nove**	*veentee-**nov***
30	**trinta**	***treen**tuh*
40	**quarenta**	*kwa**ren**tuh*
50	**cinquenta**	*seen**kwen**tuh*
60	**sessenta**	*se**sen**tuh*
70	**setenta**	*se**ten**tuh*
80	**oitenta**	*oy**ten**tuh*
90	**noventa**	*noo**ven**tuh*
100	**cem / cento**	*sayñ / **sen**too*
110	**cento e dez**	***sen**too ee desh*
500	**quinhentos**	*keen-**yen**toosh*
1,000	**mil**	*meel*
2,000	**dois mil**	*doysh meel*
1 million	**um milhão**	*ooñ meel-**yowñ***

1st	**primeiro** *pree**may**roo*
2nd	**segundo** *se**goon**doo*
3rd	**terceiro** *ter**say**roo*
4th	**quarto** ***kwar**too*
5th	**quinto** ***keen**too*
6th	**sexto** ***sesh**-too*
7th	**sétimo** ***set**imo*
8th	**oitavo** *oy**tah**-voo*
9th	**nono** ***noh**-noo*
10th	**décimo** ***dess**imoo*

AN APPOINTMENT	**UM ENCONTRO**
OPERATOR	**A TELEFONISTA**

I'd like to speak to the office manager
Queria falar com o/a gerente do escritório
__kree__-uh fa__lar__ koñ oo/uh juh-__rent__ doo shkree-__tor__-yoo

What is your address?
Qual é a sua morada?
kwal e uh __soo__-uh moo__rah__-duh

Which floor?
Em que andar?
ayñ kee an__dar__

Can you photocopy this for me?
Pode-me fotocopiar isto?
__pod__-muh foto-koop-__yar eesh__too

Do you use a courier service?
Usam serviço de mensageiro?
oo__zowñ__ ser__vee__soo duh mensa-__jay__-roo

Can you send this for me?
Pode-me mandar isto?
__pod__-muh man__dar eesh__too

What time does the office open / close?
A que horas abre / fecha o escritório?
uh kuh __or__uz __ah__-bruh / __fay__shuh oo shkree-__tor__-yoo

How do I get to your office?
Como se vai para o seu escritório?
__koh__-moo suh vy pro __say__oo shkree-__tor__-yoo

■ YOU MAY HEAR

Faça o favor de se sentar
__fah__-suh oo fa__vor__ duh suh sen__tar__
Please take a seat

...ainda não chegou
...a__een__-duh nowñ shuh__goh__
...isn't in yet

...vai atender dentro de momentos
...vy aten__dehr den__troo duh moo__men__-toosh
...will be with you in just a moment

■ BUSINESS–MEETING ■ FAX ■ LETTERS

AMOUNT TO BE PAID	A QUANTIA A PAGAR
BILL	A CONTA
CASH DESK	A CAIXA
INVOICE	A FACTURA
PAY AT THE CASH DESK	PAGUE NA CAIXA
RECEIPT	O RECIBO

How much is it?
Quanto é?
kwantoo e

How much will it be?
Quanto custará?
kwantoo kooshtuh-rah

Can I pay...?
Posso pagar...?
possoo pagar...

by credit card
com cartão de crédito
koñ kartowñ duh kreditoo

by cheque
por cheque
poor shek

Do you take credit cards?
Aceita cartões de crédito?
asaytuh kartoynsh duh kreditoo

Is service included?
O serviço está incluido?
oo serveesoo shta een-klweedoo

Is VAT included?
O IVA está incluido?
oo eevuh shta een-klweedoo

Put it on my bill
Ponha na minha conta
pon-yuh nuh meen-yuh kontuh

Please can I have a receipt
Pode-me dar um recibo por favor
pod-muh dar ooñ ruh-seeboo poor favor

Do I pay in advance?
Paga-se adiantado?
pah-guh-suh adee-an-tah-doo

Where do I pay?
Onde se paga?
onduh suh pah-guh

I'm sorry
Desculpe
dushkoolp

I've nothing smaller
Não tenho troco
nowñ ten-yoo trokoo

■ MONEY ■ SHOPPING

SUPER	**4 STAR**
SEM CHUMBO	**UNLEADED**
GASÓLEO	**DIESEL**
GASOLINA	**PETROL**
BOMBA DE GASOLINA	**PETROL PUMP**

Is there a petrol station near here?
Há alguma garagem aqui perto?
*a al**goo**muh ga**rah**-jayñ akee **pehr**too*

Fill it up, please
Encha, por favor
en**shuh poor fa**vor

Can you check the oil / the water?
Pode ver o óleo / a água?
*pod vehr oo **ol**-yoo / uh **ahg**-wuh*

...escudos worth of unleaded petrol
...escudos de gasolina sem chumbo
*...**shkoo**doosh duh gazoo-**lee**nuh sayñ **shoom**boo*

Where is...?
Onde está...?
***on**duh shta...*

the air line
o ar
oo ar

the water
a água
*uh **ahg**-wuh*

Can you check the tyre pressure, please?
Pode ver a pressão das pneus, por favor?
*pod vehr uh pruh**sowñ** dush **pnay**-oosh poor fa**vor***

Please fill this can with petrol
Por favor encha esta lata de gasolina
*poor fa**vor** **en**shuh **esh**tuh **lah**-tuh duh gazoo-**lee**nuh*

Can I pay with this credit card?
Posso pagar com o cartão de crédito?
***poss**oo pa**gar** koñ oo kar**towñ** duh **kred**itoo*

■ YOU MAY HEAR

Que bomba usou?
*kuh **bom**buh oo**zoh***
Which pump did you use?

■ BREAKDOWNS ■ CAR

FARMÁCIA *(green cross)*	PHARMACY / CHEMIST
FARMÁCIA DE SERVIÇO	DUTY CHEMIST
RECEITA MÉDICA	PRESCRIPTION

I don't feel well
Não me sinto bem
*nowñ muh **seen**too bayñ*

Have you something for...?
Tem alguma coisa para...?
*tayñ al**goo**muh **koy**-zuh **pa**ruh...*

a headache
a dor de cabeça
*uh dor duh ka**beh**-suh*

car sickness
o enjoo
*oo en**joh**-oo*

diarrhoea
a diarreia
*uh dee-uh-**ray**uh*

I have a rash
Tenho uma irritação de pele
***ten**-yoo **oo**muh eer-reetuh-**sowñ** duh pel*

Is it safe for children?
Pode-se dar às crianças?
***pod**-suh dar ash kree-**an**sush*

How much should I give?
Quanto devo dar?
***kwan**too **deh**-voo dar*

■ **YOU MAY HEAR**

Três vezes por dia antes / com / depois das refeições
*tresh **veh**-zush poor **dee**-uh antsh / koñ / duh**poysh** dush ruh-fay-**soynsh***
Three times a day before / with / after meals

■ **WORDS YOU MAY NEED**

antiseptic	**o antiséptico**	*antee**sep**tikoo*
aspirin	**a aspirina**	*ashpee**ree**nuh*
condoms	**os preservativos**	*pruhzerva**tee**voosh*
cotton wool	**o algodão**	*algoo**dowñ***
dental floss	**o fio dental**	***fee**yoo den**tal***
deodorant	**o desodorizante**	*dez-oh-dooree-**zant***
plasters	**os adesivos**	*aduh-**zee**voosh*
sanitary pads	**os pensos higiénicos**	***pen**soosh eej-**yen**ikoosh*
tampons	**os tampões**	*tam**poynsh***
toothpaste	**a pasta de dentes**	***pash**tuh duh dentsh*

■ BODY ■ DOCTOR

Tapes for video cameras and camcorders can be bought in photography shops, department stores and hypermarkets.

Where can I buy tapes for a video camera?
Onde posso comprar cassettes para a câmara de video?
***on**duh **poss**oo kom**prar** ka**setsh pa**ruh uh **ka**-maruh duh **veed**-yoo*

A colour film
Um rolo a cores
*ooñ **roh**-loo uh **kor**ush*

with 24 / 36 exposures
com 24 / 36 fotos
*koñ veentee-**kwa**troo / treentuh-**saysh fo**tosh*

A video tape for this video camera
Uma cassette para esta câmara de video
***oom**uh ka**set pa**ruh **esh**tuh **ka**-maruh duh **veed**-yoo*

Have you batteries...?
¿Tem pilhas...?
*tayñ **peel**-yush...*

for this camera
para esta máquina
***pa**ruh **esh**tuh **mak**inuh*

Can you develop this film?
Pode revelar este rolo?
*pod ruh-vuh-**lar** aysht **roh**-loo*

How much will it be?
Qual é o preço?
*kwal e oo **pray**-soo*

I'd like mat / glossy prints
Quero as cópias em mate / com brilho
***kehr**oo ush **kop**-yush ayñ mat / koñ **breel**-yoo*

When will the photos be ready?
Quando estão prontas as fotos?
***kwan**doo shtowñ pron**tush** ush **fo**tosh*

The film is stuck
O rolo não anda
*oo **roh**-loo nowñ **an**duh*

Can you take it out for me?
Pode tirá-lo por favor?
*pod tee**rah**-loo poor fa**vor***

Is it OK to take pictures here?
Posso tirar fotos aqui?
poss**oo tee**rar fo**tosh a**kee

Would you take a picture of us, please?
Pode-nos tirar uma fotografia, por favor?
pod**-noosh tee**rar oom**uh footoogruh-**fee**-uh poor fa**vor

■ SHOPPING

Main Post Offices are open from 0900 to 1700, Mon.-Fri., and until 1300 on Saturdays. Check times in small towns.

POST OFFICE	**CORREIOS**
POSTBOX	**O MARCO DO CORREIO**
STAMPS	**OS SELOS**

Is there a post office near here?
Há algum correio aqui perto?
*a al**gooñ** koo**ray**oo a**kee** **pehr**too*

Which counter sells stamps?
Em que balcão vendem selos?
*ayñ kuh bal**kowñ** ven**dayñ** **se**loosh*

I want stamps for ... postcards to Great Britain
Queria selos para ... postais para a Grã-Bretanha
***kree**-uh **se**loosh **pa**ruh ... poosh-**tysh** pra grambruh-**tahn**-yuh*

I want to send this letter registered post
Queria mandar esta carta registada
***kree**-uh man**dar** **esh**tuh **kar**tuh rujeesh-**tah**-duh*

How much is it to send this parcel?
Quanto custa mandar este embrulho?
***kwan**too **koosh**tuh man**dar** aysht aym-**brool**-yoo*

by air
por avião
*poor av-**yowñ***

first class
por correio azul
*poor koo**ray**oo a**zool***

It's a gift
É um presente
*e ooñ pruh-**zent***

The value of contents is ... escudos
O valor do conteúdo é ... escudos
*oo va**lor** doo kont-**yoo**doo e ... **shkoo**doosh*

■ YOU MAY HEAR

Preencha este impresso
*pree-**en**shuh aysht eem**press**oo*
Fill in this form

■ DIRECTIONS

Can you help me?
Pode-me ajudar?
pod-muh ajoodar

I only speak a little Portuguese
Só falo um pouco de português
so fah-loo ooñ pohkoo duh poortoo-gesh

Does anyone here speak English?
Há aqui alguém que fale inglês?
a akee algayñ kuh fah-luh eenglesh

What's the matter?
Que se passa?
kuh suh passuh

I would like to speak to whoever is in charge
Queria falar com o encarregado
kree-uh falar koñ oo aynkuh-ray-gah-doo

I'm lost
Perdi-me
perdee-muh

How do I get to...?
Como se vai a...?
koh-moo suh vy uh...

I've missed...
Perdi...
perdee...

my train
o meu comboio
oo mayoo komboyoo

my connection
a minha ligação
uh meen-yuh leeguh-sowñ

I've missed my flight because there was a strike
Perdi o meu voo porque havia uma greve
perdee oo mayoo voh-oo poorkuh avee-uh oomuh grev

The coach has left without me
O autocarro partiu sem mim
oo owtoo-karroo partyoo sayñ meeñ

Can you show me how this works?
Pode-me mostrar como funciona isto?
pod-muh mostrar koh-moo foonss-yonuh eeshtoo

I have lost my purse
Perdi o meu porta-moedas
perdee oo mayoo portuh-mway-dush

I need to get to...
Preciso de ir a...
pre-seezoo deer uh...

Leave me alone!
Deixe-me em paz!
day-shu-muh ayñ pash

Go away!
Vá-se embora!
vah-suh aymboh-ruh

■ COMPLAINTS ■ EMERGENCIES

Do you have...?
Tem...?
tayñ...

When...?
Quando...?
***kwan**doo...*

At what time...?
A que horas...?
*uh kee **or**uz...*

Where is / are...?
Onde está / estão...?
***on**duh shta / shtowñ...*

Can I...?
Posso...?
***poss**oo...*

May we...?
Podemos...?
*poo**deh**-moosh...*

Is it...?
É...? / Está...?
e... / shta...

Are they...?
São...? / Estão...?
sowñ... / shtowñ...

Is / Are there...?
Há...?
a...

Is it far?
É longe?
e lonj

What time is it?
Que horas são?
*kee **or**ush sowñ*

Who are you?
Quem é você?
*kayñ e **voh**-se*

Who...?
Quem...?
kayñ...

What...?
O quê...?
oo kay...

Why...?
Porquê...?
poorkay...

How many...?
¿Quantos(as)...?
***kwan**toosh(ush)...*

How much is it?
Quanto é?
***kwan**too e*

How...?
Como...?
***koh**-moo...*

Which one?
Qual?
kwal

Where are the toilets?
Onde são as casas de banho?
***on**duh sowñ ush **kah**-zush duh **ban**-yoo*

SAPATEIRO	SHOE REPAIR SHOP
REPARAÇÕES RÁPIDAS	REPAIRS WHILE YOU WAIT

This is broken
Isto está partido
***eesh**too shta par**tee**doo*

Where can I get this repaired?
Onde posso arranjar isto?
***on**duh **poss**oo arran**jar eesh**too*

Is it worth repairing?
Vale a pena arranjar?
*va**luh pay**nuh arran**jar***

Can you repair...?
Pode-me arranjar...?
***pod**-muh arran**jar**...*

these shoes
estes sapatos
***aysh**tush sa**pah**-toosh*

my watch
o relógio
*oo ruh-**loj**-yoo*

How much will it be?
Quanto vai custar?
kwan**too vy koosh**tar

Can you do it straightaway?
Pode fazer imediatamente?
*pod fa**zehr** eemudee-**ah**-tuh-ment*

How long will it take to repair?
Quanto tempo leva a arranjar?
kwan**too **tem**poo **leh**va arran**jar

When will it be ready?
Quando estará pronto?
***kwan**doo shtuh-**rah pron**too*

Where can I have my shoes reheeled?
Onde posso pôr capas nos sapatos?
***on**duh **poss**oo por **kah**push noosh sa**pah**-toosh*

I need some...
Preciso de...
*pre-**see**zoo duh...*

glue
cola
***ko**luh*

Sellotape®
fitacola
***fee**tuh-koluh*

string
cordel
*koor**del***

Do you have a needle and thread?
Tem uma agulha e linha?
*tayñ **oo**muh a**gool**-yuh ee **leen**-yuh*

The lights have fused
As lâmpadas fundiram-se
*ush **lahm**-padush foon**dee**rowñ-suh*

■ BREAKDOWNS

Come in!
Entre!
entruh

Please come back later
Volte mais tarde, por favor
*volt mysh tard poor fa**vor***

I'd like breakfast in my room
Queria o pequeno-almoço no quarto
***kree**-uh oo puh-**kay**noo al**moh**-soo noo **kwar**too*

Please bring...
Por favor traga-me...
*poor fa**vor** **trah**-guh-muh...*

a glass
um copo
*ooñ **kop**oo*

clean towels
toalhas limpas
***twal**-yush **leem**push*

toilet paper
papel higiénico
*pa**pel** eej-**yen**ikoo*

I'd like an early morning call tomorrow
Queria que me chamassem cedo amanhã de manhã
kree**-uh kuh muh sha**mah**-sayñ **say**-doo aman-**yañ** duh man-**yañ

At 6 o'clock
Às seis horas
*ash sayz **or**ush*

At 6.30
Às seis e meia
*ash saysh ee **may**uh*

At 7 o'clock
às sete horas
*ash se**tee** **or**ush*

I'd like an outside line
Queria uma linha exterior
kree**-uh **oom**uh **leen**-yuh shtuh-ree-**or

The ... doesn't work
O/A ... não funciona
*oo/uh ... nowñ foonss-**yo**nuh*

Please can you repair it
Pode arranjá-lo(-la), por favor
*pod arran**jah**-loo(-luh) poor fa**vor***

I need more coat hangers
Preciso de mais cabides
*pre-**see**zoo duh mysh ka**bee**dush*

Do you have a laundry service?
Tem serviço de lavandaria?
*tayñ ser**vee**soo duh lavanduh-**ree**-uh*

■ HOTEL ■ LAUNDRY ■ TELEPHONE

SALDO/DESCONTOS/LIQUIDAÇÃO	**SALE/REDUCTIONS/CLOSING-DOWN SALE**
HOJE, ABERTO ATÉ ÀS...	**OPEN TODAY UNTIL...**

How do I/we get to the main shopping area?
Como se vai para a zona comercial principal?
__koh__-moo suh vy __pa__ruh uh __zoh__-nuh koomersee-__al__ preensee-__pal__

I'm looking for a present for...
Estou à procura de um presente para...
shtoh a pro__koo__ruh dooñ pre__zent__ __pa__ruh...

a child
uma criança
__oom__uh kree-__an__suh

Where can I buy...?
Onde posso comprar...?
__on__duh __poss__oo kom__prar__...

toys
brinquedos
breen__kay__-doosh

gifts
brindes
__breen__-dush

Can you recommend any good shops?
Pode-me recomendar algumas lojas boas?
__pod__-muh ruh-koomen__dar__ al__goo__mush __lo__jush __boh__-ush

Which floor are shoes on?
Em que andar estão os sapatos?
ayñ kee an__dar__ shtowñ oosh sa__pah__-toosh

I'd like something similar to this
Queria alguma coisa parecida com isto
__kree__-uh al__goo__muh __koy__-zuh paruh-__see__duh koñ __eesh__too

It's too expensive for me
É muito caro para mim
e __mweent__oo __kah__-roo __pa__ruh meeñ

Have you anything else?
Tem alguma outra coisa?
tayñ al__goo__muh __oh__-truh __koy__-zuh

Is there a market?
Há algum mercado?
a al__gooñ__ mer__kah__-doo

Which day?
Em que dia?
ayñ kuh __dee__-uh

■ YOU MAY HEAR

Que deseja?
kuh de__zay__juh
Can I help you?

Mais alguma coisa?
mysh al__goo__muh __koy__-zuh
Would you like anything else?

■ CLOTHES ■ MEASUREMENTS & QUANTITIES

Many shops still close for lunch between 1300-1500, but the tendency is to remain open throughout the day. Large department stores and food shops generally stay open from 0900 to 1900. Shopping centres are now very common and remain open until 2200 or even 2400.

baker's	PADARIA	*paduh-**ree**-uh*
bookshop	LIVRARIA	*leevruh-**ree**-uh*
butcher's	TALHO	***tal**-yoo*
cake shop	PASTELARIA	*pashtuh-luh-**ree**-uh*
clothes *(women's)*	ROUPA DE SENHORA	***roh**-puh duh sun-**yor**uh*
clothes *(men's)*	ROUPA PARA HOMEM	***roh**-puh **pa**ruh **om**ayñ*
electrical goods	ELECTRO-DOMÉSTICOS	*ee**le**tro-doo-**mesh**tikoosh*
fishmonger's	PEIXARIA	*pay-shuh-**ree**-uh*
furniture	MOBILIÁRIO	*moobeel-**ya**-ree-oo*
gifts	BRINDES	***breen**-dush*
glasses	ÓCULOS	***oh**-kooloosh*
greengrocer's	FRUTARIA	*frootuh-**ree**-uh*
grocer's	MERCEARIA	*mersee-uh-**ree**-uh*
hairdresser's	CABELEIREIRO(A)	*kuh-buh-lay-**ray**-roo(-ruh)*
household *(goods)*	ARTIGOS DE MÉNAGE	*ar**tee**goosh duh may**naj***
ironmonger's	CASA DE FERRAGENS	***kah**-zuh duh fe**rah**-jaynsh*
jeweller's	JOALHARIA	*jwal-yuh-**ree**-uh*
lenses	LENTES	*lentsh*
market	MERCADO	*mer**kah**-doo*
optician	OCULISTA	*okoo**leesh**-tuh*
pharmacy	FARMÁCIA	*far**mass**-yuh*
self-service	AUTO-SERVIÇO	*ow**too**-ser**vee**soo*
shoe shop	SAPATARIA	*sapatuh-**ree**-uh*
shop	LOJA	***loj**uh*
stationer's	PAPELARIA	*papuluh-**ree**-uh*
supermarket	SUPER-MERCADO	*sooper-mer**kah**-doo*
sweet shop	CONFEITARIA	*konfaytuh-**ree**-uh*
tobacconist's	TABACARIA	*tabuh-ka**ree**-uh*
toy shop	LOJA DE BRINQUEDOS	***loj**uh duh breen**kay**-doosh*

The tourist office is called ***Turismo****. If you are looking for somewhere to stay they should have details of hotels, campsites, etc.*

Where is the tourist office?
Onde é o turismo?
__on__duh e oo too__reej__-moo

What can we visit in the area?
Que podemos visitar nesta zona?
kuh poo__deh__-moosh veezee__tar__ __nesh__-tuh __zoh__-nuh

When can we visit the...?
Quando podemos visitar o/a...?
__kwan__doo poo__deh__-moosh veezee__tar__ oo/uh...

We'd like to go to...
Gostariamos de ir a...
gooshtuh-__ree__-uhmoosh duh eer uh...

Have you any leaflets?
Tem alguns folhetos?
tayñ al__goonsh__ fool-__yet__oosh

Are there any excursions?
Há algumas excursões?
a al__goo__mush shkoor-__soynsh__...

When does it leave?
A que horas parte?
uh kee __or__ush part

Where does it leave from?
De onde parte?
dee __on__duh part

How much does it cost to get in?
Quanto custa a entrada?
__kwan__too __koosh__tuh uh ayn__trah__-duh

Are there any reductions for...?
Fazem descontos para...?
fah__zayñ__ dush__kon__toosh __pa__ruh...

children
crianças
kree-__an__sush

students
estudantes
shtoo__dantsh__

unemployed
desempregados
duh-zaympruh-__gah__-doosh

senior citizens
terceira idade
ter__say__ruh ee__dahd__

■ ENTERTAINMENT ■ MAPS, GUIDES & NEWSPAPERS

ABERTO
OPEN

ÁGUA PARA BEBER/ ÁGUA POTÁVEL
DRINKING WATER

AVARIADO
OUT OF ORDER

AUTO-SERVIÇO
SELF-SERVICE

BANCO *(hospital)*
CASUALTY DEPT.

BANHEIRO
LIFEGUARD *(beach)*

BILHETEIRA
TICKET OFFICE

CAIXA
CASH DESK

CASAS DE BANHO
BATHROOMS

CAVE
BASEMENT

CHEIO
FULL

COMPLETO
NO VACANCIES

DEGUSTAÇÃO
TASTING

DEPÓSITO DE BAGAGENS
LEFT LUGGAGE

DESCONTOS
REDUCTIONS

EQUITAÇÃO
HORSE RIDING

FECHADO
CLOSED

FUMADORES
SMOKING

EMPURRE
PUSH

ENTRADA
ENTRANCE

HOMENS
GENTLEMEN

IMPEDIDO
ENGAGED

INFORMAÇÕES
INFORMATION

LAVABOS
TOILETS

LIQUIDAÇÃO TOTAL
CLOSING DOWN SALE

LIVRE
VACANT/FREE

NÃO FUNCIONA
OUT OF ORDER

NÃO MEXER/ NÃO TOCAR
DO NOT TOUCH

OCUPADO
ENGAGED/OCCUPIED

PAGAR NA CAIXA
PAY AT CASH DESK

PARA ALUGAR
FOR HIRE/RENT

PARA VENDA
FOR SALE

PARTICULAR
PRIVATE

PERIGO
DANGER

PRIMEIROS SOCORROS
FIRST AID

PROIBIDO
FORBIDDEN/NO...

PUXE
PULL

QUENTE
HOT

RÉS-DO-CHÃO
GROUND FLOOR

SALDOS
SALES

SENHORAS
LADIES

VAGAS/VAGO
VACANCIES/VACANT

VESTIÁRIOS
CHANGING ROOMS

MATCH / GAME	O DESAFIO / O JOGO
PITCH / COURT	O CAMPO
TO DRAW A MATCH	EMPATAR
TO WIN	GANHAR

Where can I/we...?
Onde se pode...?
__on__duh suh pod...

play tennis
jogar ténis
*joo**gar** **tay**-neesh*

play golf
jogar golfe
*joo**gar** golf*

go swimming
nadar
*na**dar***

go jogging
fazer footing
*fa**zehr** footiñ*

see some football
ver futebol
*vehr foot**bol***

How much is it per hour?
Quanto é por hora?
***kwan**too e poor **or**uh*

Do you have to be a member?
É preciso ser sócio?
*e pre-**see**zoo sehr **soss**-yoo*

Do they hire out...?
Alugam ...?
*aloo**gowñ**...*

rackets
raquetes
*ra**ket**ush*

golf clubs
tacos de golfe
***tah**-koosh duh golf*

We'd like to go to see *(name team)* **play**
Queriamos assistir ao jogo de...
***kree**uh-moosh aseesh**teer** ow **joh**-goo duh...*

Where can we get tickets?
Onde podemos comprar bilhetes?
on**duh poo**deh**-moosh kom**prar** beel-**yetsh

How do we get to the stadium?
Como se vai para o estádio?
***koh**-moo suh vy pro **shtad**-yoo*

Which is your favourite football team? *(familiar)*
Qual é a tua equipa favorita de futebol?
*kwal e uh **too**-uh ee**kee**puh favoo**ree**tuh duh foot**bol***

What sports do you play? *(familiar)*
Que desportos praticas?
*kuh dushpor**toosh** pra**tee**kush*

■ LEISURE/INTERESTS ■ WALKING

PRAÇA DE TAXIS	TAXI RANK

I need a taxi
Preciso de um táxi
*pre-**see**zoo dooñ **tax**ee*

Where can I/we get a taxi?
Onde se pode arranjar um táxi?
***on**duh suh pod arran**jar** ooñ **tax**ee*

Please order me a taxi
Por favor chame-me um táxi
*poor fa**vor** **sha**-muh-muh ooñ **tax**ee*

now
agora
*a**gor**uh*

for...(time)
para as...
***pa**ruh ush...*

How much will it cost by taxi...?
Quanto custa ir de táxi...?
***kwan**too **koosh**tuh eer duh **tax**ee...*

to the centre
ao centro
*ow **sen**troo*

to the station
à estação
*a shta**sowñ***

to the airport
ao aeroporto
*ow uh-ehroo-**por**too*

to this address
a esta morada
*uh **esh**tuh moo**rah**-duh*

Please take me to...
Por favor leve-me a...
*poor fa**vor** **lev**-muh uh...*

Please take us to...
Por favor leve-nos a...
*poor fa**vor** **lev**-noosh uh...*

How much is it?
Quanto é?
***kwan**too e*

Why are you charging me so much?
Porque está a pedir tanto?
***poor**kuh shta uh pe**deer** **tan**too*

It's more than on the meter
É mais do que marca no contador
*e mysh doo kuh **mar**kuh noo kontuh-**dor***

Keep the change
Guarde o troco
*gward oo **tro**koo*

Sorry, I don't have any change
Desculpe, não tenho troco
*dush**koolp** nowñ **ten**-yoo **tro**koo*

I'm in a hurry
Tenho muita pressa
***ten**-yoo **mween**tuh **press**uh*

Is it far?
É longe?
e lonj

I have to catch...
Tenho que apanhar...
***ten**-yoo kuh apan-**yar**...*

the ... o'clock flight to...
o voo das ... horas para...
*oo **voh**-oo dush ... **or**ush **pa**ruh...*

■ BUS ■ METRO

*To phone Portugal from the UK, the international code is **00 351** plus the Portuguese area code (e.g. Lisbon-**1**, Oporto-**2**) followed by the number you require. To phone the UK from Portugal, dial **0044** plus the UK area code less the first 0, e.g., London (0)**171** or (0)**181**.*

PHONECARD	O CARTÃO CREDIFONE
TELEPHONE DIRECTORY	A LISTA TELEFÓNICA
YELLOW PAGES	AS PÁGINAS AMARELAS
ANSWERING MACHINE	O GRAVADOR DE CHAMADAS
COLLECT CALL	A CHAMADA A COBRAR NO DESTINO
DIAL THE NUMBER	MARCAR O NÚMERO
TO PICK UP / TO HANG UP	ATENDER / DESLIGAR

I want to make a phone call
Quero fazer uma chamada telefónica
__keh__roo fa__zehr__ __oom__uh sha__mah__-duh tuh-luh-__fon__ikuh

What coins do I need?
Que moedas preciso?
kuh __mway__-dush pre-__see__zoo

Can you show me how this phone works?
Pode-me indicar como trabalha este telefone?
__pod__-muh eendee__kar__ __koh__-moo tra__bal__-yuh aysht tuh-luh-__fon__

Where can I buy a phonecard?
Onde posso comprar um cartão Credifone?
__on__duh __poss__oo kom__prar__ ooñ kar__towñ__ kredee-__fon__

Senhor Lopes, please
O Sr. Lopes, por favor
oo sun-__yor__ lopsh poor fa__vor__

Extension...*(number)*
Extensão...
shten__sowñ__...

Can I speak to...?
Posso falar com...?
__poss__oo fa__lar__ koñ...

I would like to speak to...
Queria falar com...
__kree__-uh fa__lar__ koñ...

This is Jim Brown
Daqui Jim Brown
da__kee__ jim brown

Speaking
É o próprio / É a própria *(fem.)*
e oo __prop__ree-oo / e uh __prop__ree-uh

I will call back later
Chamo mais tarde
__sha__moo mysh tard

I will call back tomorrow
Chamo amanhã
__sha__moo aman-__yañ__

We were cut off
A chamada caíu
uh sha__mah__-duh ka__yoo__

I can't get through
Não consigo ligar
nowñ kon__see__goo lee__gar__

■ YOU MAY HEAR

Estou / Alô / Sim
shtoh / a__loh__ / seeñ
Hello

Quem fala?
kayñ __fah__-luh
Whom am I talking to?

Um momento
ooñ mo__men__-too
Just a moment

Não desligue
nowñ duj-__leeg__
Hold on

Fale, por favor
__fah__-luh poor favor
Speak now, please

Está impedido
shta eempuh-__dee__doo
It's engaged

Pode chamar mais tarde?
pod sha__mar__ mysh tard
Can you try again later?

Quer deixar um recado?
kehr day__shar__ ooñ re__kah__-doo
Do you want to leave a message?

...está em reunião
...shta ayñ ree-oo-__nyowñ__
...is in a meeting

É engano
e ayn-__guh__-noo
You've made a mistake

Não é este número
nowñ e aysht __noo__meroo
It's not this number

O telefone está avariado
oo tuh-luh-__fon__ shta avuh-ree-__ah__-doo
The telephone is out of order

Este é o gravador de chamadas de...
aysht e oo grava__dor__ duh sha__mah__-dush duh...
This is the answering machine of...

Por favor deixe a sua mensagem depois do sinal
poor fa__vor day__-shuh uh __soo__-uh men__sah__-jayñ duh-__poysh__ doo see__nal__
Please leave a message after the tone

■ BUSINESS–MEETING ■ FAX ■ OFFICE

REMOTE CONTROL	O TELECOMANDO
SOAP	A TELENOVELA
VIDEO RECORDER	O VIDEO
NEWS	O NOTICIÁRIO
TO SWITCH ON	LIGAR
TO SWITCH OFF	DESLIGAR
PROGRAMME	O PROGRAMA
CARTOONS	OS DESENHOS ANIMADOS

Where is the television?
Onde está o televisor?
__on__duh shta oo tuh-luh-vee__zor__

How do you switch it on?
Como se liga?
koh-__moo__ suh __lee__guh

Which button do I press?
Que botão uso?
kuh boo__towñ__ __oo__zoo

Please could you lower the volume?
Por favor pode reduzir o volume?
poor fa__vor__ pod ruhdoo__zeer__ oo voo-__loo__-muh

May I turn the volume up?
Posso aumentar o volume?
__poss__oo owmen__tar__ oo voo-__loo__-muh

What's on television?
Que há na televisão?
kee a nuh tuh-luh-vee__zowñ__

When is the news?
Quando são as notícias?
__kwan__doo sowñ ush noo-__teess__-yush

Do you have any English-speaking channels?
Há alguns canais em inglês?
a al__goonsh__ ka__naysh__ ayñ een__glesh__

When are the children's programmes?
Quando são os programas para crianças?
__kwan__doo sowñ oosh proo__grah__-mush __pa__ruh kree-__an__sush

Do you have any English videos?
Tem alguns videos em inglês?
tayñ al__goonsh__ __veed__-yoosh ayñ een__glesh__

PLAY	A PEÇA DE TEATRO
SEAT	O LUGAR
CLOAKROOM	O VESTIÁRIO

What's on at the theatre?
Qual é o programa de teatro?
*kwal e oo proo**grah**-muh duh tee-**ah**-troo*

What prices are the tickets?
Quais são os preços dos bilhetes?
*kwaysh sowñ oosh **pray**-soosh doosh beel-**yetsh***

I'd like two tickets...
Queria dois bilhetes...
***kree**-uh doysh beel-**yetsh**...*

for tonight
para esta noite
***pa**ruh **esh**tuh noyt*

for tomorrow night
para amanhã à noite
***pa**ruh aman-**yañ** a noyt*

for 5th August
para cinco de Agosto
***pa**ruh **seen**koo da**gosh**too*

in the stalls
na plateia
*nuh pla**tay**-uh*

in the circle
no balcão
*noo bal**kowñ***

in the upper circle
no segundo balcão
*noo se**goon**doo bal**kowñ***

How long is the interval?
Quanto dura o intervalo?
***kwan**too **doo**-ruh oo eenter-**vah**-loo*

Is there a bar?
Há um bar?
a ooñ bar

When does the performance begin / end?
Quando começa / acaba o espectáculo?
***kwan**doo koo**mess**uh / a**kah**-buh oo shpe-**tak**ooloo*

I enjoyed the play
Gostei muito da peça
*goosh**tay** **mween**too duh **peh**-suh*

It was very good
Foi muito boa
*foy **mween**too **boh**-uh*

I didn't like it at all
Não gostei nada
*Nowñ goosh-**tay** **nah**-duh*

■ ENTERTAINMENT ■ LEISURE/INTERESTS

The 24-hour clock is used a lot more than in Britain. After 1200 midday, it continues: **1300– treze horas**, **1400– catorze horas**, **1500– quinze horas**, etc, until **2400– vinte e quatro horas (meia-noite)**. With the 24-hour clock, the words **quarto** (quarter) and **meia** (half) aren't used:

1315 *(1.15pm)*	**treze e quinze**
1930 *(7.30pm)*	**dezanove e trinta**
2245 *(10.45pm)*	**vinte e duas e quarenta e cinco**

What time is it?
Que horas são?
*kee **or**ush sowñ*

am
da manhã
*duh man-**yañ***

pm
da tarde
duh tard

It's ...
São...
sowñ...

2 o'clock
duas horas
***doo**-uz **or**ush*

3 o'clock
três horas
*trez **or**ush*

6 o'clock *(etc.)*
seis horas
*sayz **or**ush*

It's 1 o'clock
É uma hora
*e **oom**uh **or**uh*

It's 1200 midday
É meio-dia
*e **may**oo **dee**-uh*

At midnight
À meia-noite
*a **may**uh noyt*

9 **nove horas**
*no**vee** **or**ush*

9.10 **nove e dez**
*no**vee** desh*

9.15 **nove e um quarto**
*no**vee** ooñ **kwar**too*

9.20 **nove e vinte**
*no**vee** veent*

9.30 **nove e trinta / nove e meia**
*no**vee** **treen**tuh / no**vee** **may**uh*

9.35 **nove e trinta e cinco / vinte e cinco para as dez**
*no**vee** **treen**tuh ee **seen**koo / veen**tee** **seen**koo **pa**ruh ush desh*

9.45 **dez menos um quarto / nove e quarenta e cinco**
*desh **may**-nooz ooñ **kwar**too / no**vee** kwa**ren**tuh ee **seen**koo*

9.50 **dez para as dez / nove e cinquenta**
*desh **pa**ruh ush desh / no**vee** seenk**wen**tuh*

When does it open / close?
Quando abre / fecha?
***kwan**doo **ah**-bruh / **fay**shuh*

When does it begin / finish?
Quando começa / acaba?
***kwan**doo koo**mess**uh / a**kah**-buh*

at 3 o'clock
às três horas
*ash trez **or**ush*

before 3 o'clock
antes das três
antsh dush tresh

after 3 o'clock
depois das três
*de**poysh** dush tresh*

today
hoje
ohj

tonight
esta noite
***esh**tuh noyt*

tomorrow
amanhã
*aman-**yañ***

yesterday
ontem
***on**tayñ*

the day before yesterday
anteontem
*antee-**on**tayñ*

the day after tomorrow
depois de amanhã
*duh-**poysh** daman-**yañ***

in the morning
de manhã
*duh man-**yañ***

this morning
esta manhã
esh**tuh man-**yañ

in the afternoon *(until dusk)*
de tarde
duh tard

in the evening *(after dusk)*
à noite
a noyt

at half past 7
às sete e meia
*ash se**tee may**uh*

at about 10 o'clock
à volta das dez horas
*a **vol**tuh dush dez **or**ush*

in an hour's time
dentro de uma hora
***den**troo **doom**uh **or**uh*

in a while
daqui a bocado
*duh**kee** uh boo**kah**-doo*

two hours ago
há duas horas
*a **doo**-ush **or**ush*

soon
em breve
ayñ brev

early
cedo
***sed**oo*

late
tarde
tard

later
mais tarde
mysh tard

I'll do it...
vou fazer...
*voh fa**zehr**...*

as soon as possible
o mais depressa possível
*oo mysh duh-**press**uh poo-**see**-vel*

...at the latest
...o mais tardar
*...oo mysh tar**dar***

■ **NUMBERS**

There are two types of train ticket for all trains: **primeira classe** *and* **segunda classe** *(1st and 2nd class). On longer trips, where it is advisable to book ahead (* **reservar lugares** *), trains may be called* **Rápidos** *(fast),* **Intercidades** *and* **Alfa** *(both intercity, modern fast trains). These trains depart from the* **Santa Apolónia** *station in Lisbon and go northwards. To travel south from Lisbon by train you must first cross the Tagus by ferry, making it far easier (and cheaper) to go by coach. Ask for details of departures at the Tourist Office. Commuter trains for the Lisbon area depart from the* **Rossio** *station (for the Sintra line) and from* **Cais do Sodré** *(for the Estoril line).*

CP *(Caminhos de Ferro Portugueses)*	**PORTUGUESE NATIONAL RAILWAYS**
SUPLEMENTO	**SUPPLEMENT PAYABLE**

When is the next train to....?
Quando é o próximo comboio para...?
***kwan**doo e oo **pross**imoo kom**boy**oo **pa**ruh...*

A single ticket
Um bilhete de ida
*ooñ beel-**yet dee**duh*

Two return tickets
Dois bilhetes de ida e volta
*doysh beel-**yetsh dee**duh ee voltuh*

to...
para...
***pa**ruh...*

First / Second class
Primeira / Segunda classe
*pree**may**ruh / se**goon**duh klas*

Smoking / No smoking
Fumador / Não fumador
*fooma**dor** / nowñ fooma**dor***

Is there a supplement to pay?
Paga-se suplemento?
***pah**-guh-suh soopluh-**men**too*

I want to book a seat on the ALFA to Aveiro
Queria reservar um lugar no ALFA para Aveiro
***kree**-uh ruh-zer**var** ooñ loo**gar** noo **al**fa **pa**ruh a**vay**roo*

Which is the first / the last train to...?
Qual é o primeiro / o último comboio para...?
*kwal e oo pree**may**roo / oo **ool**timoo kom**boy**oo **pa**ruh...*

When does it arrive in...?
A que horas chega a...?
*uh kee **or**ush **sheh**-guh uh...*

Do I have to change?
Tenho que mudar?
ten-yoo kuh moodar

Where?
Onde?
onduh

How long is there to get the connection?
Que tempo leva para a ligação?
kuh tempoo levuh paruh uh leeguh-sowñ

Which platform does it leave from?
De que plataforma parte?
duh kuh platuhformuh part

Is this the right platform for the train to...?
É esta a plataforma do comboio para...?
e eshtuh uh platuhformuh doo komboyoo paruh...

Is this the train for...?
É este o comboio para...?
e aysht oo komboyoo paruh...

When will it leave?
A que horas parte?
uh kee orush part

Why is there a delay?
Porque é o atraso?
poorkee e oo atrah-zoo

Does the train stop at...?
O comboio pára em...?
oo komboyoo pah-ruh ayñ...

Please let me know when we get to...
Por favor diga-me quando chegarmos a...?
poor favor deeguh-muh kwandoo shuhgar-mooz uh...

Is there a buffet on the train?
Há um vagão restaurante no comboio?
a ooñ vagowñ rushtoh-rant noo komboyoo

Is this free? *(seat)*
Está livre?
shta leevruh

Excuse me
Perdão / Desculpe
puhrdowñ / dushkoolp

■ LUGGAGE

There are very few vegetarian restaurants in Portugal, and those that do exist are located in the capital or Oporto and in some towns within the Algarve

Are there any vegetarian restaurants here?
Há algum restaurante vegetariano aqui?
*a al**gooñ** rushtoh-**rant** vejuh-tuh-ree-**ah**-noo a**kee***

Do you have any vegetarian dishes?
Tem algum prato vegetariano?
*tayñ al**gooñ** **prah**-too vejuh-tuh-ree-**ah**-noo*

Do you have any dishes without meat / fish?
Tem pratos sem carne / peixe?
*tayñ **prah**-toosh sayñ karn / paysh*

What fish dishes do you have?
Que pratos de peixe tem?
*kuh **prah**-toosh duh paysh tayñ*

I'd like pasta / rice...
Queria massa / arroz...
***kree**-uh **mass**uh / a**rosh**...*

without meat
sem carne
sayñ karn

without fish
sem peixe
sayñ paysh

I don't like meat / fish
Não gosto de carne / peixe
*nowñ **gosh**too duh karn / paysh*

What do you recommend?
Que recomenda?
*kuh ruh-koo**men**duh*

Is it made with vegetable stock?
É feito com caldo vegetal?
*e **fay**-too koñ **kal**doo vejuh-**tahl***

■ **POSSIBLE DISHES**

omeleta (simples / com queijo / com cogumelos) *omelette (plain / with cheese / with mushrooms)*
ovos (estrelados / mexidos com batatas fritas) *eggs (fried / scrambled with chips)*
salada (simples / mista) *salad (green / lettuce, onion, tomato)*
tortilha à espanhola *Spanish-style omelette usuallly made with cooked vegetables rather than potato and onion*

■ **EATING OUT**

Are there any guided walks?
Há alguns passeios guiados?
*a al**goonsh** pa**say**oosh ghee-**ah**-doosh*

Do you have details?
Pode-me dar informações?
pod**-muh dar eemfoormuh-**soynsh

Do you have a guide to local walks?
Tem algum guia dos passeios locais a pé?
*tayñ al**gooñ ghee**-uh doosh pa**say**oosh loo**kysh** uh pe*

How many kilometres is the walk?
De quantos quilómetros é o passeio?
*duh **kwan**toosh kee**lom**etroosh e oo pa**say**oo*

How long will it take?
Que tempo demora?
*kuh tem**poo** duh-**mor**uh*

Is it very steep?
Tem muitas subidas?
*tayñ **mween**tush soo**bee**-dush*

I'd like to go climbing
Queria fazer alpinismo
***kree**-uh fa**zehr** alpee-**neej**moo*

Do we need walking boots?
Precisamos de botas de alpinismo?
*pre-**see**zuhmoosh duh **bot**ush dalpee-**neej**moo*

Should we take...?
Devemos levar...
*duh**veh**-moosh luh**var**...*

water
água
***ahg**-wuh*

food
comida
*ko**mee**duh*

waterproofs
impermeáveis
*eempermee-**ah**-vaysh*

a compass
uma bússola
***oom**uh **boos**ooluh*

What time does it get dark?
A que horas anoitece?
*uh kee **or**uz anoy**teh**-suh*

■ MAPS, GUIDES... ■ SIGHTSEEING & TOURIST OFFICE

CHUVEIROS / AGUACEIROS	SHOWERS
LIMPO	CLEAR
CHUVA	RAIN
NEBLINA	MIST
NEVOEIRO	FOG
NUBLADO	CLOUDY

It's sunny
Está sol
shta sol

It's raining
Está a chover
*shta uh shoo**vehr***

It's windy
Está vento
*shta **ven**too*

What a lovely day!
Que belo dia!
*kuh **bel**oo **dee**-uh*

What awful weather!
Que tempo terrível!
*kuh **tem**poo te**ree**-vel*

What will the weather be like tomorrow?
Como estará o tempo amanhã?
koh**-moo shtuh-**rah** oo **tem**poo aman-**yañ

Do you think it will rain?
Pensa que vai chover?
pen**-suh kuh vy shoo**vehr

Do I need an umbrella?
Preciso de um guarda-chuva?
*pre-**see**zoo dooñ gwarduh-**shoo**vuh*

When will it stop raining?
Quando vai parar de chover?
kwan**doo vy pa**rar** duh shoo**vehr

It's very hot
Está muito calor
*shta **mween**to ka**lor***

Do you think there will be a storm?
Pensa que vai haver uma tempestade?
pen**-suh kuh vy a**vehr** **oom**uh tempush-**tahd

What is the temperature?
Qual é a temperatura?
*kwal e uh temperuh-**too**ruh*

■ MAKING FRIENDS

In Portugal there is a very wide choice of excellent wines at very reasonable prices. **Vinho da casa** *(house wine) is generally good and even cheaper. They can normally also be supplied in half bottles.*

If you like champagne-type wines there are **espumantes** *(naturally sparkling wines) locally produced. There is* **seco** *(dry),* **meio-seco** *(medium sweet) and* **doce** *(quite sweet).*

To choose wines from a list and given the bewildering variety of brands, it is best to check whether they come from a demarcated or recommended region (with controlled production).

Vinho verde *dry, green wine (not green in colour but young and slightly sparkling) from the MINHO region. Must be drunk quite cool and is good as an aperitif or to gow with shellfish and light cold meats.*

Vinho branco seco *(dry) or* **meio-seco** *(medium-dry) white wine with more body, for cold fish and seafood dishes, from the BAIRRADA, BUCELAS, COLARES and DOURO regions.*

Vinho branco seco *white dry wine with even more body, velvety for warm and heavier fish dishes, as well as for starters, from the BORBA, DÃO, PALMELA regions.*

Vinho tinto meio-encorpado *red, medium-bodied for heavier fish dishes, like salt cod and sardines, and light meats, from the ALCOBAÇA, BORBA, COLARES, DÃO, RIBATEJO regions.*

Vinho tinto velho, encorpado *old red, full-bodied, for all red meats, from the ALENTEJO, BAIRRADA, DÃO, RIBATEJO, PALMELA regions.*

For cheese (**queijo** *) it is traditional to have the wine that accompanied the meats, if the cheese is eaten following the meal (before any other dessert). If the cheese is eaten after any sweet dessert (fruit or pudding), it is customary to have a generous wine,* **meio-doce** *or* **doce** *(medium dry or sweet) from the port, madeira or Carcavelos range.*

CONT...

The wine list, please
A lista de vinhos, por favor
*uh **leesh**tuh duh **veen**-yoosh poor fa**vor***

Can you recommend a good wine?
Pode recomendar um bom vinho?
*pod ruh-koomen**dar** ooñ boñ **veen**-yoo*

A bottle...
Uma garrafa...
*__oom__uh gar**rah**-fuh...*

A carafe...
Um jarro...
*ooñ **jar**roo...*

of the house wine
de vinho da casa
*duh **veen**-yoo duh **kah**-zuh*

of red wine
de vinho tinto
*duh **veen**-yoo **teen**too*

of white wine
de vinho branco
*duh **veen**-yoo **bran**koo*

of rosé wine
de vinho rosé
*duh **veen**-yoo roh-**zay***

of 'green' wine
de vinho verde
*duh **veen**-yoo vehrd*

of dry wine
de vinho seco
*duh **veen**-yoo **seh**-koo*

of sweet wine
de vinho doce
*duh **veen**-yoo dohss*

of a local wine
de vinho da região
*duh **veen**-yoo duh ruj-**yowñ***

What liqueurs do you have?
Que licores tem?
*kuh lee-**korsh** tayñ*

A glass of port
Um cálice de Porto
*ooñ **kah**-leesuh duh **por**too*

A glass of Boal (madeira)
Um cálice de Boal
*ooñ **kah**-leesuh duh boo-**al***

UNS

rtuguese nouns are *masculine* or *feminine*, and their gender is own by the words for **the** (**o/a**) and **a** (**um/uma**) used before em (the 'article'):

masculine		*feminine*	
o/um castelo	**the/a castle**	**a/uma mesa**	**the/a table**
os castelos/(uns) castelos		**as mesas/(umas) mesas**	
the castles/(some)castles		**the tables/(some)tables**	

is usually possible to tell whether a noun is *masculine* or *minine* by its ending: nouns ending in **-o** or **-or** are usually *asculine*, while those ending in **-a** , **-agem** , **-dade** and **-tude** end to be *feminine*. There are exceptions, however, and it's est to learn the noun and the article together.

PLURAL

Nouns ending in a vowel form the plural by adding **-s** , while those ending in a consonant usually add **-es** . The exceptions to this are words ending in an **-m** which change to **-ns** in the plural and words ending in **-l** which change to **-is** in the plural: .g. **hotel – hotéis** .

OTE: When used after the words **a to**, **de of**, **em in** and **or by**, the articles (and many other words) contract:

a + as = às *ash*	**to the**
de + um = dum *dooñ*	**of a**
em + uma = numa ***noo**muh*	**to a**
por + os = pelos ***pel**oosh*	**by the**

■ TYPES OF PORT — PORTO

Port wines offer a very wide variety, according to the occasion they are to be served. The dry and semi-dry (***seco*** *and* ***meio-seco*** *) varieties are excellent as an aperitif and should be drunk slightly chilled.*

The medium-dry and sweet (***doce*** *) varieties are fine for ending a meal or at any time.*

The designation of the colour of various port wines gives a clue to their degree of sweetness (these indications are in English on the bottle).

Full or Red *dark red, young and sweet*
Ruby *lighter red, sweet and not as young as the previous*
Tawny *amber, medium-dry or sweet and more mature*
White *paler, dry*

■ TYPES OF MADEIRA — MADEIRA

Madeira wines fall into four categories and, like the ports, are served as an aperitif or for dessert, or any other occasion, according to their sweetness and personal taste. The four categories are:

Sercial *dry, pale and light*
Verdelho *darker and richer than* ***Sercial***
Boal *richer-coloured and sweeter*
Malvasia *dark, very perfumed, full-bodied and very sweet*

■ OTHER DRINKS

Aguardente / Bagaceira *strong spirits usually drunk after a meal with coffee. There are many varieties. The best are:* ***Aguardente velha*** *and* ***Aguardente velhíssima***
Amarguinha *bitter almond liqueur made in the Algarve*
Aniz *aniseed liqueur*
Ginjinha *cherry liqueur*
Moscatel *sweet wine made in Setubal with muscat grapes*
Beirão *liqueur made of a rich blend of herbs and spices*

■ DRINKING ■ EATING OUT

What work do you do?
Em que trabalha?
*ayñ kuh tra**bal**-yuh*

Do you enjoy it?
Gosta?
***goosh**tuh*

I'm...
Sou...
soh...

a doctor
médico(a)
***med**ikoo(uh)*

a teacher
professor(a)
*proofuh-**sor**(uh)*

an engineer
engenheiro(a)
*enjun-**ay**roo(uh)*

I work in...
Trabalho em...
*tra**bal**-yoo ayñ...*

a shop
uma loja
***oom**uh **loj**uh*

a factory
uma fábrica
***oom**uh **fab**rikuh*

a bank
um banco
*ooñ **ban**koo*

I work from home
Trabalho em casa
*tra**bal**-yoo ayñ **kah**-zuh*

I'm self-employed
Trabalho por conta própria
*tra**bal**-yoo poor **kon**-tuh **pro**pree-uh*

I am unemployed
Estou desempregado(a)
*shtoh duh-zaympruh-**gah**-doo(uh)*

I don't work
Não trabalho
*nowñ tra**bal**-yoo*

It's very difficult to get a job at the moment
É muito difícil arranjar trabalho agora
*e **mween**too dee**fee**seel arran**jar** tra**bal**-yoo a**gor**uh*

What are your hours?
Qual é seu horário?
*kwal e oo **say**oo oh-**rar**-yoo*

I work from 9 to 5
Eu trabalho das nove às cinco
***ay**-oo tra**bal**-yoo dush nov ash **seen**koo*

from Monday to Friday
de segunda a sexta
*duh suh**goon**-duh uh **sesh**tuh*

How much holiday do you get?
Quanto tempo tem de férias?
***kwan**too **tem**poo tayñ duh **fehr**-yush*

What do you want to be when you grow up?
Que queres fazer quando cresceres?
*kuh **kehr**ush fa**zehr** **kwan**doo krush-**sehr**ush*

■ MAKING FRIENDS

'This', 'That', 'These', 'Those'

These depend on the gender and number of the noun they represent:

este rapaz	**this boy**	**esta rapariga**	**this girl**
estes rapazes	**these boys**	**estas raparigas**	**these girls**
esse rapaz	**that boy**	**essa rapariga**	**that girl**
esses rapazes	**those boys**	**essas raparigas**	**those girls**
aquele rapaz	**that boy** *(over there)*	**aquela rapariga**	**that girl** *(over there)*
aqueles rapazes	**those boys** *(over there)*	**aquelas raparigas**	**those girls** *(over there)*

ADJECTIVES

Adjectives normally follow the nouns they describe in Portuguese, e.g. **a maçã verde** **the green apple**. Some exceptions which precede the noun are: **muito** **much, many**; **pouco** **little, not much**; **tanto** **so much, so many**; **primeiro** **first**; **último last**; **bom** **good**; **nenhum** **no, not any**; **grande** **great, big**.

Portuguese adjectives have to reflect the gender of the noun they describe. To make an adjective feminine, **-o** endings change to **-a** , and **-or** and **-ês** change to **-ora** and **-esa** . Otherwise they generally have the same form for both genders. Thus:

masculine	*feminine*
o livro vermelho	**a saia vermelha**
the red book	**the red skirt**
o homem falador	**a mulher faladora**
the talkative man	**the talkative woman**

To make adjectives plural, follow the general rules given for nouns.

'My', 'Your', 'His', 'Her'

These words also depend on the gender and number of the following noun and not on the sex of the 'owner'.

	with masc. / with fem.	*with plural nouns*
my	**o meu / a minha**	**os meus / as minhas**
his/her/its/your	**o seu / a sua**	**os seus / as suas**
our	**o nosso / a nossa**	**os nossos / as nossas**
their/your	**o seu / a sua**	**os seus / as suas**

NOTE: Since **o seu**, **a sua**, etc can mean **his**, **her**, **your**, etc, Portuguese will often replace them with the words for **of him**, **of her**, **of you**, etc (**dele**, **dela**, **de você**, etc) in order to avoid confusion:

os livros *dela*	**her books**
os livros *de você*	**your books**
os livros *deles*	**their books**

PRONOUNS

SUBJECT		OBJECT	
I	**eu** ***ay**-oo*	**me**	**me** *muh*
you *(informal)*	**tu** *too*	**you** *(informal)*	**te** *teh*
you	**você** *voh-**se***	**you**	**o/a** *oo/uh*
he	**ele** *ayl*	**him**	**o** *oo*
she	**ela** ***e**luh*	**her**	**a** *uh*
it	**ele/ela** *ayl/**e**luh*	**it**	**o/a** *oo/uh*
we	**nós** *nosh*	**us**	**nos** *noosh*
you *(informal)*	**vocês** *voh-**sesh***	**you** *(informal)*	**os/as** *oosh/ush*
you	**vós** *vosh*	**you**	**vos** *voosh*
they *(masc.)*	**eles** ***ayl**ush*	**them** *(masc.)*	**os** *oosh*
they *(fem.)*	**elas** ***e**lush*	**them** *(fem.)*	**as** *ush*

NOTES

1. **YOU** The polite form of addressing someone would be with **o Senhor** or **a Senhora** using the **(s)he** form or the verb and the object pronoun **o/a** . The semi-formal **you** is **você** and the informal **you** is **tu** (like French and Spanish).

2. Subject pronouns are normally not used except for emphasis or to avoid confusion:

_eu_ vou para Lisboa e _ele_ vai para Coimbra
_I_'m going to Lisbon and _he_'s going to Coimbra

3. Object pronouns are usually placed after the verb and joined with a hyphen:

vejo-_o_	**I see him**

However, in sentences beginning with a 'question word' or a 'negative word' the pronoun goes in front of the verb:

quando _o_ viu?	**when did you see him?**
não _o_ vi	**I did not see him**

Also, in sentences beginning with **that** and **who**, etc ('subordinate clauses') the pronoun precedes the verb:

sei que _o_ viu	**I know that you saw him**
o homem que _o_ viu	**the man who saw him**

4. **Me** also = **to me** and **nos** = **to us**, but **lhe** = **to him/to her/to it/to you** *(formal)*, **te** = **to you** *(informal)* and **lhes** = **to them/to you**.

5. When two pronouns are used together they are often shortened. The verb will also change spelling if it ends in **-r** , **-s** , **-z** or a nasal sound:

dá-mo	**(= dá + me + o)**	**he gives me it**
dê-lho	**(= dê + lhe + o)**	**give him it**
fá-lo	**(= faz + o)**	**he does it**
dão-nos	**(= dão + os** *or* **dão + nos)**	**they give them** *or* **they give us**

6. The pronoun following a preposition has the same form as the subject pronoun, except for **mim** (**me**), **si** (**you** – *formal*), **ti** (**you** – *informal*).

VERBS

There are three main patterns of endings for verbs in Portuguese – those ending **-ar**, **-er** and **-ir** in the dictionary.

CANTAR	TO SING	COMER	TO EAT
canto	**I sing**	como	**I eat**
cantas	**you sing**	comes	**you eat**
canta	**(s)he/it sings/you sing**	come	**(s)he/it eats/you eat**
cantamos	**we sing**	comemos	**we eat**
cantais	**you sing**	comeis	**you eat**
cantam	**they/you sing**	comem	**they/you eat**

PARTIR	TO LEAVE
parto	**I leave**
partes	**you leave**
parte	**(s)he/it leaves/you leave**
partimos	**we leave**
partis	**you leave**
partem	**they/you leave**

And in the past tense:

cantei	**I sang**	comi	**I ate**
cantaste	**you sang**	comeste	**you ate**
cantou	**(s)he/it/you sang**	comeu	**(s)he/it/you ate**
cantámos	**we sang**	comemos	**we ate**
cantastes	**you sang**	comestes	**you ate**
cantaram	**they/you sang**	comeram	**they/you ate**

parti	**I left**
partiste	**you left**
partiu	**(s)he/it/you left**
partimos	**we left**
partistes	**you left**
partiram	**they/you left**

Four of the most common verbs are irregular:

SER	TO BE	ESTAR	TO BE
sou	**I am**	estou	**I am**
és	**you are**	estás	**you are**
é	**(s)he/it is/you are**	está	**(s)he/it is/you are**
somos	**we are**	estamos	**we are**
sois	**you are**	estais	**you are**
são	**they/you are**	estão	**they/you are**

TER	TO HAVE	IR	TO GO
tenho	**I have**	vou	**I go**
tens	**you have**	vais	**you go**
tem	**(s)he/it has/you have**	vai	**(s)he/it goes/you go**
temos	**we have**	vamos	**we go**
tendes	**you have**	ides	**you go**
têm	**they/you have**	vão	**they/you go**

NOTE: **Ser** and **Estar** both mean **to be**.

Ser is used to describe a permanent place or state:

sou inglês	**I am English**
é uma praia	**it is a beach**

Estar is used to describe a temporary state or where something is located:

como está?	**how are you?**
onde está a praia?	**where is the beach?**

DICTIONARY
ENGLISH-PORTUGUESE
PORTUGUESE-ENGLISH

a	**um (uma)**
abbey	**a abadia**
about	**cerca de**
about ten o'clock	*por volta das dez*
above	**acima de; por cima de**
abroad adj	**no estrangeiro**
go abroad	*ir ao estrangeiro*
absence	**a ausência**
accelerator	**o acelerador**
accent	**o acento**
(pronunciation)	**a pronúncia**
accept	**aceitar ; aprovar**
acceptable	**aceitável ; satisfatório(a)**
accident	**o acidente**
accommodation	**o alojamento**
account	**a conta**
accountant	**o/a contabilista**
accuracy	**a exactidão**
accustomed	**acostumado(a) ; habituado(a)**
ache	**a dor**
I have a headache	*dói-me a cabeça*
acknowledge	**admitir ; reconhecer**
acknowledgement	**a confirmação ; a resposta**
acquire	**adquirir ; obter**
act *n*	**o acto**
act *vb*	**actuar ; agir**
adapt	**adaptar ; ajustar**
adaptor *(electrical)*	**o adaptador**
add	**adicionar ; juntar**
addict	**o/a viciado(a)**
address	**a morada**
what is your address?	*qual é a sua morada?*
address book	**a agenda**
adhesive tape	**a fita adesiva**

adjust	**ajustar ; arranjar**
admission charge	**o preço de entrada**
adult	**o/a adulto(a)**
advance: ***in advance***	***antecipadamente***
advertisement	**o anúncio**
afraid	**medroso(a)**
I am afraid	***tenho medo***
African	**africano(a)**
after	**depois**
afternoon	**a tarde**
again	**outra vez**
against *prep*	**contra**
age	**a idade**
old age	***a idade avançada***
agent	**o/a agente**
ago: ***2 days ago***	***há 2 dias***
agreement	**o acordo**
ahead *adv*	**adiante**
aid	**a ajuda**
AIDS	**o SIDA**
air conditioning	**o ar condicionado**
airline	**a linha aérea**
air mail	**a via aérea**
air mattress	**o colchão pneumático**
airport	**o aeroporto**
aisle *(plane, theatre, etc)*	**a coxia**
alarm	**o alarme**
alarm clock	**o despertador**
alcoholic *adj*	**alcoólico(a)**
all	**todo(a), todos(as)**
allergic	**alérgico(a)**
alley	**a travessa**
all right	**está bem**
are you all right?	***você está bem?***

almond	**a amêndoa**
almost	**quase**
also	**também**
always	**sempre**
am	*see* **GRAMMAR**
ambulance	**a ambulância**
America	**a América**
American	**americano(a)**
anaesthetic	**o anestésico**
anchor	**a âncora**
and	**e**
angry	**zangado(a)**
another	**um(a) outro(a)**
another beer?	*mais uma cerveja?*
answer *n*	**a resposta**
answer *vb*	**responder**
answering machine	**o gravador de chamadas**
antibiotic	**o antibiótico**
antifreeze	**o anticongelante**
antiques	**as antiguidades**
antiseptic	**o antiséptico**
any: *have you any apples?*	*tem algumas maçãs?*
anybody	**qualquer pessoa**
anything	**qualquer coisa**
apartment	**o apartamento**
apple	**a maçã**
appointment	**o encontro ; a consulta**
apricot	**o damasco**
are	*see* **GRAMMAR**
arm	**o braço**
arrest *vb*	**prender**
arrival	**a chegada**
arrive	**chegar**

art gallery	**o museu de arte**
arthritis	**a artrite**
artichoke	**a alcachofra**
article	**o artigo**
ashtray	**o cinzeiro**
asparagus	**o espargo**
aspirin	**a aspirina**
assistance	**a assistência**
asthma	**a asma**
at	**em**
at home	*em casa*
attack	**o ataque**
heart attack	*o ataque de coração*
attractive (person)	**atraente**
aubergine	**a beringela**
aunt	**a tia**
automatic	**automático(a)**
autumn	**o outono**
average	**a média**
avocado	**o abacate**
award	**o prémio**
awful	**terrível**
baby	**o bebé**
baby food	**a comida de bebé**
baby-sitter	**o/a babysitter**
bachelor	**o solteiro**
back	**as costas**
back ache	*a dor de costas*
back seat	*o assento traseiro*
backpack	**a mochila**
bacon	**o toucinho**
bad	**estragado(a) ; mau (má)**

badge	**o emblema**
bag	**o saco ; a mala**
baggage	**a bagagem**
baggage reclaim	**a recolha de bagagem**
bail	**a fiança**
bait *(for fishing)*	**a isca**
baker's	**a padaria**
balcony	**a varanda**
bald *(person)*	**calvo(a)**
(tyre)	**careca**
ball	**a bola**
banana	**a banana**
band	**a banda musical**
bandage	**a ligadura**
bank	**o banco**
bar	**o bar**
barber	**o barbeiro**
basket	**o cesto**
basketwork	**os cestos ; os artigos de vime**
bath	**o banho**
take a bath	***tomar banho***
bathing cap	**a touca de banho**
bathroom	**a casa de banho**
battery *(for car)*	**a bateria**
(for torch, radio, etc)	**a pilha**
be	*see* **GRAMMAR**
beach	**a praia**
bean	**o feijão**
beautiful	**belo(a)**
bed	**a cama**
bedding	**a roupa de cama**
bedroom	**o quarto**
beef	**a carne de vaca**
beer	**a cerveja**

beetroot	**a beterraba**
before	**antes de**
begin	**começar**
behind	**atrás**
believe	**acreditar**
bell *(door)*	**a campaínha**
below	**por baixo de**
belt	**o cinto**
beside	**ao lado de**
best	**o/a melhor**
better (than)	**melhor (do que)**
between	**entre**
bicycle	**a bicicleta**
big	**grande**
bigger	**maior**
bill	**a conta**
bin	**o caixote do lixo**
binoculars	**os binóculos**
bird	**o pássaro**
birthday	**o aniversário**
birthday card	**o cartão de aniversário**
biscuit	**a bolacha**
bit: ***a bit of***	***um bocado (de)***
bite *(insect)*	**a picada ; a mordedura**
bitten	**mordido(a) ; picado(a)**
bitter	**amargo(a)**
black	**preto(a)**
blackcurrant	**a groselha**
blank	**o espaço vazio/em branco**
blanket	**o cobertor**
bleach	**a lixívia**
blind *adj (person)*	**cego(a)**
blind *n (for window)*	**a persiana**

blocked	**bloqueado(a)**
blood	**o sangue**
blood group	**o grupo sanguíneo**
blouse	**a blusa**
blow-dry	**o brushing**
blue	**azul**
boarding card	**o cartão de embarque**
boarding house	**a pensão**
boat	**o barco**
boat trip	**a viagem de barco**
body	**o corpo**
boiled	**cozido(a)**
boiling	**em ebulição**
bone	**o osso**
book *n*	**o livro**
book of tickets	*a caderneta de bilhetes*
book *vb*	**reservar**
booking	**a marcação**
booking office	**a bilheteira**
bookshop	**a livraria**
boots	**as botas**
border	**a fronteira**
boring	**maçador(a) ; aborrecido(a)**
boss	**o/a chefe ; o/a patrão/patroa**
both	**ambos(as)**
bottle	**a garrafa**
bottle-opener	**o abre-garrafas**
box	**a caixa**
box office	**a bilheteira**
boy	**o rapaz**
boyfriend	**o namorado**
bra	**o soutien**
bracelet	**a pulseira**

brain	o cérebro
brake fluid	o óleo dos travões
brakes	os travões
branch *(of tree)*	o ramo
(of business, etc)	a sucursal
brandy	o conhaque
bread	o pão
break	partir ; quebrar
breakable	frágil
breakdown	a avaria
breakdown service	*o pronto-socorro*
breakfast	o pequeno-almoço
breast	o peito ; o seio
breathe	respirar
brick	o tijolo
bride	a noiva
bridge	a ponte
briefcase	a pasta
bright	brilhante
brine	a salmoura
bring	trazer
Britain	a Grã-Bretanha
British	britânico(a)
broad	largo(a)
brochure	a brochura
broken	partido(a)
broken down *(car, etc)*	avariado(a)
broom	a vassoura
brother	o irmão
brown	castanho(a)
brush	a escova
bucket	o balde
budget	o orçamento
buffet	o bufete

buffet car	**o vagão restaurante**
building	**o edifício**
bulb *(light)*	**a lâmpada**
bureau de change	**a casa de câmbio**
burglar	**o ladrão**
burglary	**o roubo**
burn *n*	**a queimadura**
burn *vb*	**queimar**
burst	**rebentado(a)**
bus	**o autocarro**
bus station	*a estação de autocarros*
bus stop	*a paragem de autocarros*
bus tour	*a excursão de autocarro*
business	**os negócios**
busy	**ocupado(a)**
but	**mas**
butcher's	**o talho**
butter	**a manteiga**
button	**o botão**
buy	**comprar**
by	**perto de ; por ; ao lado de**
bypass	**o desvio**
cab	**o táxi**
café	**o café**
cake	**o bolo**
calamine lotion	**a loção de calamina**
calculator	**a calculadora**
calendar	**o calendário**
call *vb*	**chamar**
call *n*	**uma chamada**
a long-distance call	*uma chamada interurbana*
camcorder	**a camcorder**

camera	**a máquina fotográfica**
camp	**acampar**
camp site	**o parque de campismo**
can *vb*	**poder**
can *n*	**a lata**
canned goods	*as conservas*
cancel	**cancelar**
candle	**a vela**
canoe	**a canoa**
can-opener	**o abre-latas**
capable	**competente**
car	**o carro**
carafe	**a garrafa ; o jarro**
caravan	**a caravana**
card *(greetings)*	**o cartão**
(playing)	**a carta de jogar**
careful	**cuidadoso(a)**
carnation	**o cravo**
car park	**o parque de estacionamento**
carpet	**a carpete**
carriage	**a carruagem**
carrot	**a cenoura**
carry	**transportar**
car wash	**a lavagem automática**
case	**a mala**
cash *n*	**o dinheiro**
cash desk	**a caixa**
cassette	**a cassette**
castle	**o castelo**
cat	**o gato**
catch *(bus, train, etc)*	**apanhar**
cathedral	**a catedral**
cave	**a caverna**
cd	**o disco compacto**

cd player	**o leitor de discos compactos**
cemetery	**o cemitério**
centimetre	**o centímetro**
central	**central**
centre	**o centro**
century	**o século**
certain	**certo(a)**
certificate	**o certificado ; a certidão**
chain	**a corrente**
chair	**a cadeira**
champagne	**o champanhe**
change *n (loose coins)*	**o troco**
change *vb*	**trocar ; mudar**
changing room	**o gabinete de provas**
chapel	**a capela**
charge	**o custo**
cover charge	*o custo do serviço*
charm	**o encanto**
cheap	**barato(a)**
cheaper	**mais barato(a)**
check	**verificar**
check in	**fazer o check-in**
check-in desk	**o balcão do check-in**
cheerful	**bem disposto(a) ; alegre**
cheers	**saúde!**
cheese	**o queijo**
chemist's	**a farmácia**
cheque	**o cheque**
cheque book	**o livro de cheques**
cheque card	**o cartão de cheques**
cherry	**a cereja**
chest *(of body)*	**o peito**
chestnut	**a castanha**

chewing gum	a pastilha elástica
chicken	a galinha
chickenpox	a varicela
child	a criança
children	as crianças
chilli	a malagueta
chips	as batatas fritas
chocolate	o chocolate
chocolates	os chocolates
choice	a escolha
chop *(meat)*	a costeleta
Christmas	o Natal
church	a igreja
cider	a cidra
cigar	o charuto
cigarette	o cigarro
cinema	o cinema
circuit	o circuito ; a volta
circus	o circo
city	a cidade
claim *n*	a reclamação
clap	bater palmas
clean *adj*	limpo(a)
clean *vb*	limpar
client	o/a cliente
climb	subir
climbing	o alpinismo
climbing boots	as botas de alpinismo
cloakroom	o vestiário
clock	o relógio
close *adj*	perto
close *vb*	fechar
closed	fechado(a)

cloth *(fabric)*	**o tecido**
clothes	**as roupas**
clothes peg	**a mola da roupa**
cloudy	**nublado(a)**
clove *(spice)*	**o cravinho**
club	**o clube**
coach	**o autocarro ; a carruagem**
coach trip	**a viagem de autocarro**
coast	**a costa ; o litoral**
coastguard	**a polícia marítima**
coat	**o casaco**
coat hanger	**o cabide**
cocoa	**o cacau**
coconut	**o coco**
coffee	**o café**
white coffee	***o café com leite ; o galão***
black coffee	***o café***
coin	**a moeda**
Coke ®	**a coca cola**
colander	**o coador**
cold *n*	**o frio**
cold *adj*	**frio(a)**
I'm cold	***tenho frio***
colour	**a cor**
comb	**o pente**
come	**vir ; chegar**
come in!	***entre!***
(come back)	**voltar**
(come in)	**entrar**
comfortable	**confortável**
comment *n*	**o comentário**
comment *vb*	**comentar**
communion	**a comunhão**
company	**a companhia**

compartment	**o compartimento**
complain	**queixar-se (de)**
compliment	**o elogio**
compliments	*os cumprimentos*
compulsory	**obrigatório(a)**
computer	**o computador**
concern *(worry)*	**a preocupação**
I am concerned	*estou preocupado(a)*
concert	**o concerto**
condition *(requirement)*	**a condição**
(state)	**o estado**
conditioner	**o acondicionador**
condom	**o preservativo**
conductor *(bus, etc)*	**o cobrador ; o condutor**
conference	**a conferência**
confession	**a confissão**
confirm	**confirmar**
congratulations!	**parabéns!**
connection	**a ligação**
constipated	**com prisão de ventre**
consulate	**o consulado**
contact lens cleaner	**o líquido para as lentes de contacto**
contact lenses	**as lentes de contacto**
container	**o recipiente**
contraceptive	**o preservativo; o anticoncepcional**
cook	**cozinhar**
cooker	**o fogão**
cool	**fresco(a)**
cool box *(for picnics)*	**a caixa refrigerada**
copy *n*	**a cópia**
copy *vb*	**copiar**
coriander	**os coentros**

corkscrew **o saca-rolhas**
corner **o canto**
cost *n* **o custo**
cost *vb* **custar**
how much does it cost? *quanto custa?*
cotton **o algodão**
cotton wool **o algodão (hidrófilo)**
couchette **a couchette**
cough **a tosse**
counter *(shop, bar, etc))* **a balcão**
country **o campo ; o país**
couple **o casal**
courier **o guia turístico**
(to send package) **o mensageiro**
course *(of meal)* **o prato**
(of study) **o curso**
cow **a vaca**
crab **o caranguejo**
craftsman **o artesão**
crash **o choque**
crash helmet **o capacete**
cream *(for face, etc)* **o creme**
(on milk) **a nata**
credit card **o cartão de crédito**
crisis **a crise**
crisps **as batatinhas fritas**
crop **a colheita**
cross **cruzar**
crossed lines **as linhas cruzadas**
crossroads **a encruzilhada ; o cruzamento**
crowd **a multidão**
crowded **cheio(a) de gente**
cruet-stand **o galheteiro**
cruise **o cruzeiro**

crumb	a migalha
cry *n (shout)*	o grito
cry *vb (weep)*	chorar
cucumber	o pepino
cultivate	cultivar
cup	a chávena
cupboard	o aparador ; o armário
currant	a passa de corinto
current	a corrente
curtain	a cortina
cushion	a almofada
custard	a custarda ; o leite-creme
customer	o freguês/a freguesa
customs	a alfândega
cut *n*	o corte
cut *vb*	cortar
we've been cut off	*foi interrompida a ligação*
cutlery	os talheres
cycle	a bicicleta
cycling	o ciclismo

daily	cada dia ; diariamente
damage *n*	os danos
damp	húmido(a)
dance *n*	o baile
dance *vb*	dançar
dangerous	perigoso(a)
dark	escuro(a)
date	a data
date of birth	a data de nascimento
daughter	a filha
dawn	a madrugada

day	o dia
dead	morto(a)
deaf	surdo(a)
dear	caro(a) ; querido(a)
death	a morte
debt	a dívida
decaffeinated coffee	o café descafeinado
deceit	o engano
deck chair	a cadeira de lona
declare	declarar
deep	fundo(a)
defrost	descongelar
delay	a demora
delicatessen	a charcutaria
delicious	delicioso(a)
demand	a exigência
dentist	o/a dentista
dentures	a dentadura postiça
deodorant	o desodorizante
department store	o grande armazém
departure lounge	a sala de embarque
departures	as partidas
deposit	o depósito
dessert	a sobremesa
details	os pormenores
detergent	o detergente
detour	o desvio
develop	desenvolver
diabetic	diabético(a)
dialling code	o código
diamond	o diamante
diarrhoea	a diarreia
diary	o diário

dictionary	**o dicionário**
diesel	**o gasóleo**
diet	**a dieta**
I'm on a diet	***estou a fazer dieta***
different	**diferente**
difficult	**difícil**
dinghy	**o bote**
dining room	**a sala de jantar**
dinner	**o jantar**
direct	**directo(a)**
directory *(telephone)*	**a lista telefónica**
directory enquiries	**as informações telefónicas**
dirty	**sujo(a)**
disabled *(person)*	**o/a deficiente**
disappear	**desaparecer**
disappointed	**desiludido(a)**
disaster	**o desastre**
disco	**a discoteca**
discount	**o desconto**
disease	**a doença**
dish	**o prato**
dishwasher	**a máquina de lavar louça**
disinfectant	**o desinfectante**
display *n*	**a exposição**
display *vb*	**expor ; mostrar**
distance	**a distância**
distilled water	**a água destilada**
disturbance	**a perturbação ; a desordem**
divorced	**divorciado(a)**
dizzy	**tonto(a)**
do	**fazer**
doctor	**o/a médico(a)**
documents	**os documentos**

dog *(male)*	**o cão**
(female)	**a cadela**
doll	**a boneca**
dollar	**o dólar**
donkey	**o burro**
door	**a porta**
double	**o dobro**
double bed	**a cama de casal**
double room	**o quarto de casal**
doubt *n*	**a dúvida**
doubt *vb*	**duvidar**
down	**para baixo**
go down	*descer*
downstairs	**em baixo**
drain	**o cano ; o esgoto**
draught *(of air)*	**a corrente de ar**
drawer	**a gaveta**
drawing	**o desenho**
dress *n*	**o vestido**
dress (oneself)	**vestir-se**
dressing *(for food)*	**o tempero ; o molho**
drill *(tool)*	**a broca**
drink *n*	**a bebida**
drink *vb*	**beber**
drinking water	**a água potável**
drive	**conduzir**
driver	**o/a condutor(a)**
driving licence	**a carta de condução**
drizzle	**o chuvisco**
drought	**a seca**
drown	**afogar**
drunk	**embriagado(a)**
drug	**o medicamento ; a droga**

dry *adj*	**seco(a)**
dry *vb*	**secar**
dry-cleaner's	**a limpeza a seco**
duck	**o pato**
dummy *(for baby)*	**a chupeta**
during	**durante**
dust *n*	**o pó**
duty-free shop	**o duty-free**
duvet	**o edredão**
dynamo	**o dínamo**

each	**cada**
ear	**a orelha**
earache	**as dores de ouvidos**
earlier	**mais cedo**
early	**cedo**
ear-phones	**os auscultadores**
earrings	**os brincos**
earth *(planet)*	**a terra**
earthquake	**o terramoto**
east	**o leste**
Easter	**a Páscoa**
easy	**fácil**
eat	**comer**
echo	**o eco**
edge	**a beira ; a aresta**
effective	**eficaz**
egg	**o ovo**
fried egg	***o ovo estrelado***
hard-boiled egg	***o ovo cozido***
scrambled eggs	***os ovos mexidos***
elastic band	**o elástico**
electric	**eléctrico(a)**

electrician	o/a electricista
electricity	a electricidade
electricity meter	o contador de electricidade
electric razor	a máquina de barbear
elegant	elegante
embarrassing	embaraçoso(a)
embassy	a embaixada
emergency	a emergência
employment	o emprego ; o trabalho
empty	vazio(a)
end	o fim
engaged *(to be married)*	comprometido(a)
(phone, toilet, etc)	ocupado(a)
engine	o motor
engineer	o/a engenheiro(a)
England	a Inglaterra
English	inglês (inglesa)
enjoy oneself	divertir-se
I enjoy swimming	*gosto de nadar*
enlarge	aumentar
enormous	enorme
enough	bastante
enquiry desk	o balcão de informações
enter	entrar
entertainment	a diversão
entrance	a entrada
entrance fee	o bilhete de entrada
envelope	o envelope
equipment	o equipamento
error	o erro
escalator	a escada rolante
escape *vb*	escapar ; fugir
escape ladder	a escada de salvação

especially	**especialmente**
establish	**estabelecer**
Eurocheque	**o Eurocheque**
Europe	**a Europa**
eve	**a véspera**
Christmas Eve	*a véspera de Natal*
evening	**a noite**
in the evening	*à noite*
evening meal	**o jantar**
every	**cada**
everyone	**toda a gente**
everything	**todas as coisas**
examination	**o exame**
example	**o exemplo**
excellent	**excelente**
except	**excepto**
excess luggage	**o excesso de bagagem**
exchange *vb*	**trocar**
exchange rate	**o câmbio**
exciting	**excitante**
excursion	**a excursão**
excuse	**a desculpa**
excuse me!	*desculpe!*
exhaust pipe	**o tubo de escape**
exhibition	**a exposição**
exit	**a saída**
expense	**a despesa**
expensive	**caro(a)**
expert	**o/a perito(a)**
expire *(ticket, etc)*	**caducar ; expirar**
explain	**explicar**
extinguish	**apagar**
eye	**o olho**

fabric	**o tecido**
face	**a cara**
facilities	**as instalações**
factory	**a fábrica**
faint	**desmaiar**
fair *(hair)*	**louro(a)**
fake	**falso(a)**
fall	**cair**
he/she has fallen	*ele/ela caíu*
family	**a família**
famous	**famoso(a)**
fan *(hand-held)*	**o leque**
(electric)	**a ventoínha**
fan belt	**a correia da ventoinha**
far	**longe**
fare *(train, bus, etc)*	**o preço (da passagem)**
farm	**a quinta**
farming	**a agricultura**
fashion	**a moda**
fast	**rápido(a)**
fat	**gordo(a)**
father	**o pai**
father-in-law	**o sogro**
fault *(defect)*	**o defeito**
it's not my fault	*a culpa não é minha*
favourite	**favorito(a)**
feather	**a pena**
feed	**alimentar**
feel	**apalpar ; sentir**
I feel sick	*tenho náuseas*
fellow	**o companheiro**
ferry	**o ferry-boat**
festival	**o festival**
fetch	**trazer ; ir buscar**

fever	**a febre**
few	**poucos(as)**
a few	*alguns (algumas)*
fiancé(e)	**o/a noivo(a)**
field	**o campo**
fig	**o figo**
fight	**a briga**
file *(nail)*	**a lima**
filigree	**a filigrana**
fill (up)	**encher**
fill it up!	*encha o depósito!*
fillet	**o filete**
film *(at cinema)*	**o filme**
(for camera)	**o rolo de películas**
filter	**o filtro**
find	**achar**
fine *n (to be paid)*	**a multa**
fine *adj*	**fino(a) ; excellent**
fine arts	*as belas-artes*
finish	**acabar**
fire	**o fogo**
fire brigade	**os bombeiros**
fire extinguisher	**o extintor**
fireworks	**os fogos de artifício**
first	**o/a primeiro(a)**
first aid	**os primeiros socorros**
first class	**de primeira classe**
first floor	**o primeiro andar**
first name	**o nome próprio**
fish *n*	**o peixe**
fish *vb*	**pescar**
fisherman	**o pescador**
fishing rod	**a cana de pesca**
fit *vb* **:** ***it doesn't fit me***	*não me fica bem*

fit *n*	**o ataque**
he had a fit	*ele teve um ataque*
fix	**reparar**
fizzy	**gasoso(a)**
flag	**a bandeira**
flash	**o flash**
flask	**o termo**
flat *n (apartment)*	**o apartamento**
flat *adj*	**plano(a)**
flat tyre	**o furo**
flaw	**a falha**
flea	**a pulga**
flight	**o voo**
flippers	**as barbatanas**
flood	**a inundação**
floor	**o andar ; o chão**
flour	**a farinha**
flower	**a flor**
flu	**a gripe**
fly	**a mosca**
fog	**o nevoeiro**
foggy	**enevoado(a)**
foil *(silver)*	**o papel de alumínio**
follow	**seguir**
food	**a comida**
food poisoning	**a intoxicação alimentar**
fool	**tonto(a)**
foot	**o pé**
football	**o futebol**
for	**para**
foreign	**estrangeiro(a)**
forecast	**a previsão**
weather forecast	*a previsão do tempo*
foreman	**o capataz**

forest	**a floresta**
forever	**para sempre**
forget	**esquecer-se de**
forgive	**perdoar**
fork *(for eating)*	**o garfo**
(in road)	**a bifurcação**
former	**o/a anterior ; o/a precedente**
fortnight	**a quinzena**
fortress	**a fortaleza**
forward(s)	**para a frente**
fountain	**a fonte**
fox	**a raposa**
fracture *n*	**a fractura**
fragrant	**perfumado(a)**
France	**a França**
free	**livre ; grátis**
freedom	**a liberdade**
freezer	**o congelador**
French	**francês (francesa)**
french beans	**o feijão-verde**
frequent	**frequente**
fresh	**fresco(a)**
fridge	**o frigorífico**
fried	**frito(a)**
friend	**o/a amigo(a)**
frog	**a rã**
from	**de**
front	**a frente**
frozen	**congelado(a)**
fruit	**a fruta**
fruit juice	**o sumo de frutas**
fruit salad	**a salada de frutas**
fruity	**com sabor a fruta**

frying pan	**a frigideira**
fuel	**o combustível**
fuel pump	**a bomba de gasolina**
full	**cheio(a)**
full board	**a pensão completa**
fumes *(of car)*	**os fumos de escape**
funeral	**o funeral**
funfair	**o parque de diversões**
funny	**engraçado(a) ; estranho(a)**
fur	**a pele**
furniture	**a mobília**
fuse	**o fusível**

gallery	**o museu de arte**
gallon	***= approx. 4.5 litres***
game	**o jogo**
garage	**a garagem**
garden	**o jardim**
garlic	**o alho**
garnish *vb*	**guarnecer**
gas	**o gás**
gas cylinder	**a botija de gás**
gate	**o portão ; a entrada**
gear	**a velocidade**
generous	**generoso(a)**
gentleman	**o cavalheiro**
Gents'	**Homens**
genuine	**genuíno(a) ; autêntico(a)**
German	**alemão (alemã)**
German measles	**a rubéola**
Germany	**a Alemanha**

get *(obtain)*	**obter**
(receive)	**receber**
(fetch)	**ir buscar**
get my book	***vai buscar o meu livro***
get into	**entrar**
get off	**descer de**
gift	**o presente**
gift shop	**a loja de lembranças**
ginger	**o gengibre**
girl	**a rapariga**
girlfriend	**a namorada**
give	**dar**
(give back)	**devolver**
glass *(to drink out of)*	**o copo**
a glass of water	***um copo de água***
glasses	**os óculos**
gloss	**o lustro ; o brilho**
gloves	**as luvas**
glue	**a cola**
go	**ir**
(go back)	**voltar**
(go down)	**descer**
(go in)	**entrar**
(go out)	**sair**
God	**o Deus**
godchild	**o/a afilhado(a)**
goggles	**os óculos de protecção**
gold	**o ouro**
golf	**o golfe**
golf course	**o campo de golfe**
good	**bom (boa)**
good afternoon	**boa tarde**
goodbye	**adeus**
good evening	**boa noite**
good morning	**bom dia**

good night	boa noite
goose	o ganso
graduate	o/a licenciado(a)
gramme	o grama
grand	grande
grandfather	o avô
great grandfather	*o bisavô*
grandmother	a avó
great grandmother	*a bisavó*
grapefruit	a toranja
grapefruit juice	o sumo de toranja
grapes	as uvas
grass	a erva
greasy	oleoso(a) ; gorduroso(a)
great	grande
green	verde
green card *(car insurance)*	o cartão verde
grey	cinzento(a)
grilled	grelhado(a)
grocer's	a mercearia
ground *(earth)*	a terra
(floor)	o chão
ground floor	o rés-do-chão
group	o grupo
grow	crescer
guarantee	a garantia
guard	o guarda
guest	o/a convidado(a); o/a hóspede
guesthouse	a pensão
guide *n*	o/a guia
guide *vb*	guiar
guidebook	a guia
guided tour	a excursão guiada
gym shoes	os ténis

haemorrhoids	as hemorróidas
hair	o cabelo
hairbrush	a escova de cabelo
haircut	o corte de cabelo
hairdresser	o/a cabeleireiro(a)
hair dryer	o secador de cabelo
hairgrip	o gancho de cabelo
half	a metade
a half bottle of	*meia garrafa de*
half board	a meia pensão
half-price	pela metade do preço
ham	o presunto
hammer	o martelo
hand	a mão
handbag	o saco de mão
handicapped *(person)*	o/a deficiente
handkerchief	o lenço
hand luggage	a bagagem de mão
hand-made	feito(a) à mão
hangover	a ressaca
happen	acontecer
what happened?	*o que aconteceu?*
happy	feliz
harbour	o porto
hard	duro(a)
harm	o mal ; o dano
harvest	a colheita
hat	o chapéu
have	ter *see* GRAMMAR
hay fever	a febre dos fenos
hazelnut	a avelã
he	ele *see* GRAMMAR
head	a cabeça

headache	a dor de cabeça
hear	ouvir
hearing aid	o aparelho auditivo
heart	o coração
heart attack	o ataque de coração
heater	o aquecedor
heating	o aquecimento
heavy	pesado(a)
height	a altura
hello	olá ; está?
help *n*	a ajuda
help!	*socorro!*
help *vb*	ajudar
can you help me?	*pode-me ajudar?*
hepatitis	a hepatite
herb	a erva aromática
here	aqui
high	alto(a)
high blood pressure	a tensão alta
highchair	a cadeira de bebé
hill	a colina
hill-walking	o alpinismo
hire	alugar
hit	atingir ; bater
hitchhike	andar à boleia
hold *(contain)*	conter
hold-up	o engarrafamento
hole	o buraco
holiday	o feriado
on holiday	*em férias*
hollow	oco(a)
home	a casa
homesick: *be homesick*	*ter saudades*
honey	o mel

honeymoon	**a lua-de-mel**
hope	**esperar**
I hope so/not	*espero que sim/não*
hors d'œuvre	**a entrada**
horse	**o cavalo**
hose(pipe)	**a mangueira**
hospital	**o hospital**
hot	**quente**
I'm hot	*tenho calor*
it's hot	*está calor*
hotel	**o hotel**
hour	**a hora**
house	**a casa**
housekeeper	**a governanta**
house wine	**o vinho da casa**
how	**como**
how much?	*quanto?*
how many?	*quantos(as)?*
how are you?	*como está?*
hungry: ***I am hungry***	*tenho fome*
hurry: ***I'm in a hurry***	*tenho pressa*
hurt	**doer**
that hurts	*isso dói*
husband	**o marido**
I	**eu** see **GRAMMAR**
ice	**o gelo**
with ice	*com gelo*
ice cream	**o gelado**
iced	**gelado(a)**
ice lolly	**o gelado**
if	**se**
ignition	**a ignição**
ill	**doente**

I'm ill	*estou doente*
immediately	**imediatamente**
impatient	**impaciente**
important	**importante**
impossible	**impossível**
in	**dentro de**
inch	**=** *approx. 2.5 cm*
included	**incluído(a)**
increase *n*	**o aumento**
indigestion	**a indigestão**
indoors	**em casa ; dentro de casa**
inefficient	**ineficiente**
infectious	**infeccioso(a) ; contagioso(a)**
information	**a informação**
information office	**as informações**
ingredient	**o ingrediente**
injection	**a injecção**
injured	**ferido(a)**
ink	**a tinta**
insect	**o insecto**
insect bite	**a mordedura de insecto**
insect repellent	**o repelente contra insectos**
inside	**dentro**
instalment	**a prestação**
instant coffee	**o café instantâneo**
instead	**em vez de**
instructor	**o/a instrutor(a)**
insulin	**a insulina**
insurance	**o seguro**
insurance certificate	**a apólice de seguro**
interesting	**interessante**
international	**internacional**
interpreter	**o/a intérprete**

interval	**o intervalo**
interview	**a entrevista**
into	**em ; dentro**
invitation	**o convite**
invite	**convidar**
invoice	**a factura**
Ireland	**a Irlanda**
Irish	**irlandês (irlandesa)**
iron *(metal)*	**o ferro**
(for clothes)	**o ferro de engomar**
iron *vb*	**passar a ferro**
ironmonger's	**a loja de ferragens**
is	*see* GRAMMAR
island	**a ilha**
it	**o/a** *see* GRAMMAR
Italian	**italiano(a)**
Italy	**a Itália**
itch	**a comichão**
jack *(for car)*	**o macaco**
jacket	**o casaco**
jam	**a compota**
jammed *(stuck)*	**bloqueado(a)**
jar	**o jarro ; o boião**
jaundice	**a icterícia**
jealous	**ciumento(a)**
jeans	**as jeans**
jelly	**a geleia**
jellyfish	**a medusa**
jewel	**a jóia**
jewellery	**a joalharia ; a ourivesaria**
job	**o emprego**

jog	**ir fazer jogging**
joke	**a piada ; a anedota**
journalist	**o/a jornalista**
journey	**a viagem**
jug	**o jarro**
juice	**o sumo**
jump leads	**os cabos para ligar a bateria**
junction	**o cruzamento**
just: *just two*	*apenas dois*
I've just arrived	*acabo de chegar*

keep	**guardar**
kettle	**a chaleira**
key	**a chave**
keyring	**o porta-chaves**
kidneys	**os rins**
kilo	**o quilo**
kilometre	**o quilómetro**
king	**o rei**
kind *adj*	**amável ; bondoso(a)**
kiosk	**o quiosque**
kiss *vb*	**beijar**
kitchen	**a cozinha**
kitten	**o/a gatinho(a)**
knee	**o joelho**
knickers	**as cuecas**
knife	**a faca**
knot	**o nó**
know	**saber ; conhecer**

label	**a etiqueta**
lace	**a renda**
laces *(for shoes)*	**os atacadores**
ladder	**a escada**
Ladies' *(toilet)*	**Senhoras**
lady	**a senhora**
lager	**a cerveja**
lake	**o lago**
lamb	**o cordeiro**
lamp	**a lâmpada**
land	**a terra**
(country)	**o país**
landing *(of plane)*	**a aterragem**
landlady	**a senhoria**
landlord	**o senhorio**
lane *(on motorway)*	**a faixa**
language	**a língua**
large	**grande**
last	**último(a)**
last week	***a semana passada***
late	**tarde**
the train is late	***a comboio está atrasado***
sorry we are late	***desculpe o atraso***
later	**mais tarde**
launderette	**a lavandaria automática**
laundry service	**o serviço de lavandaria**
lavatory	**o lavabo**
lawyer	**o/a advogado(a)**
lazy	**preguiçoso(a)**
leader	**o guia**
leaf	**a folha**
leak	**a fuga**
learn	**aprender**
lease	**o arrendamento**

least: ***at least***	*pelo menos*
leather	**o couro ; o cabedal**
leave	**partir ; deixar**
when does it leave?	*a que horas parte?*
left: ***on/to the left***	*à esquerda*
left-luggage *(office)*	**o depósito de bagagens**
leg	**a perna**
lemon	**o limão**
lemonade	**a limonada**
lemon tea	**o carioca de limão**
lend	**emprestar**
length	**o comprimento**
lens	**a lente**
less	**menos**
lesson	**a lição**
let *(allow)*	**deixar**
(lease)	**alugar**
letter	**a carta**
(of alphabet)	**a letra**
letterbox	**o marco do correio**
lettuce	**a alface**
library	**a biblioteca**
licence *(driving)*	**a carta de condução**
lid	**a tampa**
lie down	**deitar-se**
life	**a vida**
lifeboat	**o salva-vidas**
lifeguard	**o banheiro salva-vidas**
life jacket	**o colete de salvação**
lift	**o elevador**
light	**a luz**
have you a light?	*tem lume?*
light bulb	**a lâmpada**
lighter	**o isqueiro**

lightning	**os relâmpagos**
like *prep*	**como**
it's like this	*é assim*
like *vb*	**gostar de**
I like coffee	*gosto de café*
lime	**a lima**
line	**a linha**
lip salve	**a manteiga de cacau**
lipstick	**o bâton**
listen (to)	**ouvir**
litre	**o litro**
litter *(rubbish)*	**o lixo**
little	**pequeno(a)**
a little...	*um pouco de...*
live	**viver**
he lives in London	*ele vive em Londres*
liver	**o fígado**
living room	**a sala de estar**
lizard	**o lagarto**
loaf	**o pão**
lobster	**a lagosta**
lock *vb*	**fechar com chave**
lock *n*	**a fechadura**
locker *(for luggage)*	**o depósito de bagagem**
London	**Londres**
long	**comprido(a) ; longo(a)**
for a long time	*durante muito tempo*
look	**olhar ; parecer**
(look after)	**cuidar de**
(look for)	**procurar**
lorry	**o camião**
lose	**perder**
lost	**perdido(a)**
I have lost my wallet	*perdi a minha carteira*
I am lost	*perdi-me*

lost property office	**a secção de perdidos e achados**
lot: ***a lot***	*muitos*
lotion	**a loção**
loud *(noisy)*	**barulhento(a) ; ruidoso(a)**
lounge	**a sala de estar**
love	**amar**
I love swimming	*gosto muito de nadar*
lovely	**encantador(a)**
low	**baixo(a)**
low tide	**a maré-baixa**
luck	**a sorte**
lucky	**afortunado(a)**
luggage	**a bagagem**
luggage rack	**o porta-bagagens**
luggage tag	**a etiqueta de bagagem**
luggage trolley	**o carrinho**
lunch	**o almoço**
luxury	**o luxo**

macaroni	**o macarrão**
machine	**a máquina**
madam	**a senhora**
magazine	**a revista**
maid	**a empregada**
maiden name	**o nome de solteira**
main	**principal**
main course *(of meal)*	**o prato principal**
mains *(electrical)*	**a rede eléctrica**
make	**fazer ; preparar**
make-up	**a maquilhagem**

man	**o homem**
manager	**o/a gerente**
many	**muitos(as)**
map	**o mapa**
marble	**o mármore**
margarine	**a margarina**
market	**o mercado**
marmalade	**o doce de laranja**
married	**casado(a)**
mass	**a missa**
match	**o fósforo**
(game)	**o jogo**
material	**o material**
matter: ***it doesn't matter***	***não tem importância***
meal	**a refeição**
mean	**significar**
what does this mean?	***o que significa isto?***
measles	**o sarampo**
measure	**a medida**
meat	**a carne**
mechanic	**o/a mecânico(a)**
medicine	**o medicamento**
medium	**médio(a)**
medium rare *(meat)*	***meio-passado(a)***
meet	**encontrar**
meeting	**a reunião**
melon	**o melão**
melt	**fundir ; derreter**
member *(of club, etc)*	**o sócio**
men	**os homens**
menu	**a ementa**
merchandise	**a mercadoria**
meringue	**o merengue**
message	**a mensagem**

meter	**o contador**
metre	**o metro**
microwave *(oven)*	**o micro-ondas**
midday	**o meio-dia**
midnight	**a meia-noite**
migraine	**a enxaqueca**
mile	***8 km = 5 miles***
milk	**o leite**
milk shake	**o batido de leite**
millimetre	**o milímetro**
million	**o milhão**
mince	**a carne picada**
mind *n*	**a mente**
mind *vb*	**ocupar-se de ; objectar**
do you mind?	***importa-se?***
mineral water	**a água mineral**
minimum	**o mínimo**
minister *(political)*	**o ministro**
minor road	**a estrada secundária**
mint *(sweet)*	**o rebuçado de hortelã**
minute	**o minuto**
mirror	**o espelho**
miss *(plane, train, etc)*	**perder**
Miss...	**Menina...**
missing *(thing)*	**perdido(a)**
mistake	**o erro**
misty	**enevoado(a)**
misunderstanding	**o mal-entendido**
modern	**moderno(a)**
moisturizer	**o creme hidratante**
monastery	**o mosteiro**
money	**o dinheiro**
money order	**o vale postal**

month	**o mês**
monument	**o monumento**
moon	**a lua**
mop	**a esfregona**
more	**mais**
more than three	*mais de três*
more bread	*mais pão*
morning	**a manhã**
mosquito	**o mosquito**
moth *(clothes)*	**a traça**
mother	**a mãe**
mother-in-law	**a sogra**
motor	**o motor**
motorboat	**o barco a motor**
motorcycle	**a motocicleta**
motorway	**a auto-estrada**
mountain	**a montanha**
mouse	**o rato**
mousse	**a mousse**
moustache	**o bigode**
mouth	**a boca**
Mr	**Senhor**
Mrs	**Senhora**
much	**muito(a)**
too much	*demais*
mumps	**a papeira**
muscle	**o músculo**
museum	**o museu**
mushroom	**o cogumelo**
music	**a música**
mussel	**o mexilhão**
must	**dever**
mustard	**a mostarda**
mutton	**o carneiro**

nail *(metal)* **o prego**
(on finger) **a unha**
nail polish **o verniz das unhas**
nail polish remover **a acetona**
naked **nu(a)**
name **o nome**
napkin **o guardanapo**
nappy **a fralda**
narrow **estreito(a)**
nationality **a nacionalidade**
navy blue **azul marinho**
near **perto**
necessary **necessário(a)**
neck **o pescoço**
necklace **o colar**
need **precisar de**
needle **a agulha**
a needle and thread *uma agulha e a linha*
negative *(photography)* **a película**
neighbour **o/a vizinho(a)**
nephew **o sobrinho**
never **nunca**
I never drink wine *nunca bebo vinho*
new **novo(a)**
news **a notícia**
newsagent **a tabacaria**
newspaper **o jornal**
New Year **o Ano Novo**
New Zealand **a Nova Zelândia**
next **próximo(a)**
nice **simpático(a)**
niece **a sobrinha**
night **a noite**
nightclub **a boite**

nightdress **a camisa de noite**
no **não**
nobody **ninguém**
noisy **barulhento(a)**
nonalcoholic **não-alcoólico(a)**
none **nenhum(a)**
there's none left *não sobrou nada*
non-smoking **não-fumador**
north **o norte**
Northern Ireland **a Irlanda do Norte**
nose **o nariz**
not **não**
I don't know *não sei*
note **a nota**
note pad **o bloco-notas**
nothing **nada**
now **agora**
number **o número**
number plate *(car)* **a matrícula**
nurse **o/a enfermeiro(a)**
nut *(to eat)* **a noz**
(for bolt) **a porca**

oar **o remo**
occasionally **às vezes**
octopus **o polvo**
of **de**
off *(radio, engine, etc)* **desligado(a)**
(milk, food, etc) **estragado(a)**
offer **oferecer**
office **o escritório**
often **muitas vezes**
oil **o óleo**

oil filter	o filtro do óleo
ointment	a pomada
OK	está bem
old	velho(a)
how old are you?	*que idade tem?*
olive	a azeitona
olive oil	o azeite
omelette	a omeleta
on	em
on the table	*na mesa*
once	uma vez
one	um (uma)
one-way	de sentido único
onion	a cebola
only	somente
open *adj*	aberto(a)
open *vb*	abrir
opera	a ópera
operator *(telephone)*	o/a telefonista
opposite	em frente de
or	ou
orange *adj*	cor de laranja
orange *n*	a laranja
orange juice	o sumo de laranja
order	encomendar
organize	organizar
original	original
other	o/a outro(a)
the other one	*o/a outro(a)*
ounce	*= approx. 30 g*
out	fora
he's gone out	*ele saiu*
outdoor	ao ar livre
outside	lá fora

outskirts	**os arredores**
oven	**o forno**
over	**sobre**
overcharge	**cobrar demais**
owe	**dever**
you owe me...	*deve-me...*
owner	**o/a dono(a)**
oyster	**a ostra**
pack *(bags)*	**fazer as malas**
package	**o embrulho**
package tour	**a viagem organizada**
packet	**o pacote**
paddling pool	**a piscina para crianças**
padlock	**o cadeado**
paid	**pago(a)**
pain	**a dor**
painful	**doloroso(a)**
painkiller	**o analgésico**
painting	**a pintura ; o quadro**
pair	**o par**
palace	**o palácio**
pan	**a frigideira**
pancake	**a panqueca**
pants *(briefs)*	**as cuecas**
paper	**o papel**
parcel	**a encomenda**
pardon	**desculpe?**
I beg your pardon!	*desculpe-me!*
parents	**os pais**
park *n*	**o parque**

park *vb*	estacionar
parking disk	o disco de estacionamento
parsley	a salsa
part	a parte
partner *(business)*	o/a sócio(a)
(friend)	o/a companheiro(a)
party *(celebration)*	a festa
(political)	o partido
passenger	o/a passageiro(a)
passport	o passaporte
passport control	o controle de passaportes
pasta	as massas
pastry	a massa ; o bolo
pâté	o paté
path	o caminho
pavement	o passeio
pay	pagar
payment	o pagamento
peace	a paz
peach	o pêssego
peak rate	a taxa alta
peanut	o amendoim
pear	a pêra
peas	as ervilhas
pedestrian	o/a peão
pedestrian crossing	a passadeira para peões
peel *vb (fruit)*	descascar
peg	o cabide ; a mola
pen	a caneta
pencil	o lápis
penicillin	a penicilina
penknife	o canivete
pensioner	o/a reformado(a)

pepper	a pimenta ; o pimento
per: *per hour*	*por hora*
per week	*por semana*
perfect	perfeito(a)
performance	a representação
perfume	o perfume
perhaps	talvez
period *(menstruation)*	a menstruação
perm	a permanente
permit	a licença
person	a pessoa
petrol	a gasolina
petrol station	a bomba de gasolina
pewter	o estanho
phone	*see* **telephone**
phonecard	o credifone
photocopy	a fotocópia
photograph	a fotografia
picnic	o piquenique
picture *(on wall)*	o quadro
pie	a empada ; a torta
piece	o bocado
pier	o cais
pill	o comprimido
pillow	a almofada
pillowcase	a fronha
pin	o alfinete
pineapple	o ananás
pink	cor-de-rosa
pint	*= approx. 0.5 litre*
a pint of beer	*uma caneca de cerveja*
pipe *(for smoking)*	o cachimbo
(drain, etc)	o tubo ; o cano
place	o lugar

plane	**o avião**
plaster	**o adesivo**
plastic	**o plástico**
plate	**o prato**
platform *(railway)*	**a plataforma**
play	**jogar**
playroom	**o quarto de brinquedos**
please	**por favor**
pliers	**o alicate**
plug *(electric)*	**a ficha ; a tomada**
(for sink)	**a válvula**
plum	**a ameixa**
plumber	**o canalizador**
points	**os platinados**
poisonous	**venenoso(a)**
police	**a polícia**
police officer	**o/a polícia**
police station	**a esquadra**
polish *(for shoes)*	**a pomada para o calçado**
polluted	**poluído(a)**
pollution	**a poluição**
pony trekking	**o passeio a cavalo**
pool	**a piscina**
poor	**pobre**
poorly: ***he feels poorly***	***ele não se sente bem***
popular	**popular**
pork	**a carne de porco**
port *(wine)*	**o vinho do porto**
porter *(for door)*	**o porteiro**
(for luggage)	**o carregador**
Portugal	**Portugal**
Portuguese	**português (portuguesa)**
possible	**possível**
post	**pôr no correio**

postbox	**o marco do correio**
postcard	**o postal**
postcode	**o código postal**
post office	**os correios**
pot *(for cooking)*	**a panela**
potato	**a batata**
pottery	**a cerâmica**
pound *(money)*	**a libra**
(weight)	*= approx. 0.5 kilo*
powdered milk	**o leite em pó**
prawn	**o lagostim**
prayer	**a oração**
prefer	**preferir**
pregnant	**grávida**
prepare	**preparar**
prescription	**a receita médica**
present *(gift)*	**o presente**
press *(newspapers)*	**a imprensa**
pretty	**bonito(a)**
price	**o preço**
price list	**a lista de preços**
pride	**o orgulho**
priest	**o padre**
prince	**o príncipe**
princess	**a princesa**
print *(photo)*	**a cópia**
private	**privado(a)**
prize	**o prémio**
probably	**provavelmente**
problem	**o problema**
programme	**o programa**
prohibited	**proibido(a)**
pronounce	**pronunciar**
how's this pronounced?	***como se pronuncia isto?***

prune	**a ameixa seca**
public	**público(a)**
public holiday	**o feriado**
publisher	**o/a editor(a)**
pudding	**o pudim**
pull	**puxar**
pullover	**o pulover**
pump	**a bomba**
puncture	**o furo**
puppet show	**o teatro de marionetes; os fantoches**
purple	**roxo(a)**
purse	**o porta-moedas**
push	**empurrar**
pushchair	**o carrinho**
put	**pôr**
pyjamas	**o pijama**

quality	**a qualidade**
quay	**o cais**
queen	**a rainha**
question *n*	**a pergunta**
queue	**a fila ; a bicha**
quick	**rápido(a)**
quickly	**depressa**
quiet	**sossegado(a)**
quilt	**o edredão**
quite: ***it's quite good***	***é bastante bom***
it's quite expensive	***é muito caro***
quotation (estimate)	**o orçamento**

English	Portuguese
rabbit	**o coelho**
rabies	**a raiva**
race	**a corrida**
(human)	**a raça**
racket	**a raqueta**
radio	**o rádio**
radish	**o rabanete**
raffle	**a rifa**
railway station	**a estação de comboio**
rain *n*	**a chuva**
rainbow	**o arco-íris**
raincoat	**o impermeável**
raining: ***it's raining***	***está a chover***
raisin	**a passa de uva**
rare	**raro(a)**
(steak)	**mal passado(a)**
rash *(skin)*	**a urticária**
raspberry	**a framboesa**
rate	**a taxa**
rate of exchange	***o câmbio***
raw	**cru(a)**
razor	**a máquina de barbear**
razor blades	**as lâminas de barbear**
read *(book, etc)*	**ler**
ready	**pronto(a)**
real	**real**
reason *n*	**a razão**
receipt	**o recibo**
recently	**recentemente**
reception (desk)	**a recepção**
recipe	**a receita**
recommend	**recomendar**
record	**o disco**
recover	**recuperar**

red	**vermelho(a)**
reduction	**o desconto**
refill	**a recarga**
refund	**o reembolso**
registered	**registado(a)**
regulations	**os regulamentos**
reimburse	**reembolsar**
relation	**o parente**
relax	**repousar**
reliable *(person, service)*	**de confiança**
remain	**ficar**
remember	**lembrar-se de**
rent *vb*	**alugar**
rental	**o aluguer**
repair	**reparar**
repeat	**repetir**
report *n*	**o relatório**
reservation	**a reserva**
reserve	**reservar**
reserved	**reservado(a)**
rest *n*	**o descanso ; o resto**
the rest of the wine	*o resto do vinho*
rest *vb*	**descansar**
restaurant	**o restaurante**
restaurant car	**o vagão restaurante**
retired	**reformado(a)**
return	**voltar ; devolver**
return ticket	**o bilhete de ida e volta**
reverse-charge call	**a chamada pagável no destino**
rheumatism	**o reumatismo**
rice	**o arroz**
rich *(person)*	**rico(a)**
(food)	**suculento(a)**

she	**ela** *see* **GRAMMAR**
sheep	**a ovelha**
sheet *(for bed)*	**o lençol**
shelf	**a prateleira**
shellfish	**o marisco**
sherry	**o xerez**
ship	**o barco**
shirt	**a camisa**
shock absorber	**o amortecedor**
shoe	**o sapato**
shop	**a loja**
shop assistant	**o/a vendedor(a)**
hopping: ***go shopping***	***ir às compras***
hort	**curto(a)**
ort-cut	**o atalho**
rts	**os calções**
w *n*	**o espectáculo**
vb	**mostrar**
er	**o duche**
	o chuveiro ; o aguaceiro
s	**os camarões**
	o santuário ; o relicário
(closed)	**fechado(a)**
	fechar
	as persianas ; as gelosias
	doente
	o turismo
notice, etc)	**o sinal ; a sinalização**
	a assinatura
	a seda
	a prata
	similar
	simples

ride *(horse)*	**montar a cavalo**
right *adj*	**certo(a)**
right *adv* **:** ***on/to the right***	***à direita***
ring *(for finger)*	**o anel**
ripe	**maduro(a)**
river	**o rio**
road	**a estrada**
road map	**o mapa das estradas**
roast	**assado(a)**
robber	**o ladrão**
roll *(bread)*	**o pãozinho**
roof	**o telhado**
roof rack	**o tejadilho**
room *(of house, etc)*	**o quarto**
room service	**o serviço de quarto**
rope	**a corda**
rosé	**o vinho rosé**
rotten *(fruit, etc)*	**podre ; estragado(a)**
rough *(surface)*	**áspero(a)**
round	**redondo(a)**
roundabout	**a rotunda**
route	**a rota**
rowing boat	**o barco a remos**
royal	**real**
rubber	**a borracha**
rubber band	**o elástico**
rubbish	**o lixo**
rucksack	**a mochila**
rug	**o tapete**
rush hour	**a hora de ponta**
rusty	**ferrugento(a)**

sad	triste
safe *n*	o cofre
safe *adj*	seguro(a)
safety pin	o alfinete de segurança
sail(ing)	a vela
sailboard	a prancha
salad	a salada
salad dressing	o tempero da salada
sales	o saldo
salesperson	o/a vendedor(a)
salmon	o salmão
salt	o sal
same	mesmo(a)
sand	a areia
sandals	as sandálias
sandwich	a sandes
sanitary towel	o penso higiénico
sardine	a sardinha
sauce	o molho
saucepan	a caçarola
saucer	o pires
sausage	a salsicha
savoury	saboroso(a)
savouries	os salgados
say	dizer
scarf *(headscarf)*	o lenço (de pescoço)
school	a escola
scissors	a tesoura
score *vb*	marcar
Scotland	a Escócia
Scottish	escocês (escocesa)
screw	o parafuso
screwdriver	a chave de parafusos

sculpture	a escultura
sea	o mar
seafood	o peixe e o marisco
seasickness	o enjoo
seaside	a praia
season ticket	o passe
seat *(chair)*	a cadeira
(on bus, train, etc)	o lugar
second	segundo(a)
second class	de segunda classe
second-hand	em segunda mã
see	ver
self-service	o auto-serviç
sell	vender
Sellotape ®	a fita-cola
send	mandar
senior citizen	o/a ref
separate	sepa
serious	gra
serve	se
service	
service charge	
set menu	
several	
sew	
shade *(shadow)*	
shallow	
shampoo	
shampoo and s	
share *vb*	
shave	
shaving cream	
shawl	

sing	cantar
single *(not married)*	solteiro(a)
single bed	a cama de pessoa só
single room	o quarto individual
sink	o lava-louça
sir	senhor
sister	a irmã
sit	sentar-se
size	o número
skate	o patim
skating	a patinagem
skimmed milk	o leite desnatado
skin	a pele
skirt	a saia
sky	o céu
sleep	dormir
sleeper *(on train)*	a carruagem-cama
sleeping bag	o saco cama
sleeping pill	o comprimido para dormir
slice	a fatia
slippers	os chinelos
slow	lento(a)
small	pequeno(a)
smaller	mais pequeno(a)
smell	o cheiro
smile *n*	o sorriso
smile *vb*	sorrir
smoke *n*	o fumo
smoke *vb*	fumar
smoked	fumado(a)
smooth	liso(a) ; macio(a)
snack bar	o snack-bar
snorkel	o tubo de ar

snow	**a neve**
so	**portanto**
so much	*tanto(a)*
soap	**o sabão ; o sabonete**
soap powder	**o sabão em pó**
sober	**sóbrio(a)**
sock	**a peúga**
socket (electrical)	**a tomada**
soft	**macio(a)**
soft drink	**o refrigerante**
some	**alguns (algumas)**
someone	**alguém**
something	**alguma coisa**
sometimes	**às vezes**
son	**o filho**
song	**a canção**
soon	**em breve**
sore	**magoado(a)**
sorry: ***I'm sorry!***	***lamento***
sort: ***what sort of cheese?***	***que tipo de queijo?***
soup	**a sopa**
south	**o sul**
souvenir	**a recordação**
space	**o espaço**
spade	**a enxada**
Spain	**a Espanha**
Spanish	**espanhol(a)**
spanner	**a chave inglesa**
spare wheel	**a roda sobressalente**
sparkling (wine)	**espumoso(a)**
spark plug	**a vela**
speak	**falar**
special	**especial**

speciality a especialidade
speed a velocidade
speed limit o limite de velocidade
spell: ***how do you spell it?*** *como se escreve?*
spicy picante
spinach o espinafre
sponge a esponja
spoon a colher
sport o desporto
spring *(season)* a primavera
square *(in town)* a praça
squash *(drink)* o sumo
squid as lulas
stadium o estádio
stairs a escada
stalls *(in theatre)* a plateia
stamp o selo
star *(in sky, in films)* a estrela
start começar
starter *(in meal)* a entrada
(car) o motor de arranque
station a estação
stationer's a papelaria
stay ficar
I'm staying at a hotel *fico num hotel*
steak o bife
steep íngreme
steering wheel o volante
sterling esterlino(a)
stew o guisado
steward o comissário de bordo
stewardess a hospedeira de bordo
sticking plaster o adesivo

still *(not moving)*	**imóvel**
(not sparkling)	**sem gás**
sting	**a picada**
stomach	**o estômago**
stomach upset	**o mal-estar de estômago**
stop	**parar**
storm	**a tempestade**
straight on	**sempre em frente**
straw *(for drinking)*	**a palha**
strawberry	**o morango**
street	**a rua**
street map	**o mapa das ruas**
string	**o cordel ; o fio**
strong	**forte**
stuck	**pegado(a)**
student	**o/a estudante**
stung	**picado(a)**
stupid	**estúpido(a)**
suddenly	**de repente**
suede	**a camurça**
sugar	**o açúcar**
suit	**o fato**
suitcase	**a mala**
summer	**o verão**
sun	**o sol**
sunbathe	**tomar banhos de sol**
sunbloc	**o protector solar**
sunburn	**a queimadura de sol**
sunglasses	**os óculos de sol**
sunny	**soalheiro(a)**
sunrise	**o nascer do sol ; o amanhecer**
sunset	**o pôr do sol ; o ocaso**
sunshade	**o guarda-sol ; a sombra**

sunstroke	**a insolação**
suntan lotion	**a loção de bronzear**
supermarket	**o supermercado**
supper	**a ceia**
supplement	**o suplemento**
surcharge	**a sobretaxa**
sure	**seguro(a)**
surfboard	**a prancha de surf**
surname	**o apelido**
surrounded by	**rodeado(a) por**
sweater	**o pulover**
sweet *adj*	**doce**
sweetener	**o edulcorante**
sweets	**os doces ; as guloseimas**
swim	**nadar**
swimming pool	**a piscina**
swimsuit	**o fato de banho**
swing *(for children)*	**o baloiço**
Swiss	**suíço(a)**
switch	**o interruptor**
switch off	**apagar ; desligar**
switch on	**acender ; ligar**
Switzerland	**a Suíça**
swollen *(finger, ankle, etc)*	**inchado(a)**
table	**a mesa**
tablecloth	**a toalha de mesa**
tablespoon	**a colher de sopa**
tablet	**o comprimido**
table tennis	**o ping-pong**
take	**levar ; tomar**
(take out)	**tirar ; retirar**

talc	**o talco**
talk	**conversar**
tall	**alto(a)**
tame *(animal)*	**manso(a)**
tampons	**os tampões**
tap	**a torneira**
tape	**a fita**
tape recorder	**o gravador**
tartar sauce	**o molho tártaro**
taste *vb* **:** ***can I taste some?***	***posso provar?***
taste *n*	**o sabor**
tax	**o imposto**
taxi	**o táxi**
taxi rank	**a praça de táxis**
tea	**o chá**
tea bag	**o saquinho de chá**
teach	**ensinar**
teacher	**o/a professor(a)**
teapot	**o bule**
tear *(in eye)*	**a lágrima**
(in material)	**o rasgão**
teaspoon	**a colher de chá**
teeth	**os dentes**
telephone	**o telefone**
telephone box	**a cabine telefónica**
telephone call	**a chamada**
telephone directory	**a lista telefónica**
television	**a televisão**
television set	**o televisor**
tell	**dizer**
temperature	**a temperatura**
(have a temperature)	***ter febre***
temporary	**temporário(a)**
tennis	**o ténis**

tennis ball	**a bola de ténis**
tennis court	**o campo de ténis**
tennis racket	**a raqueta de ténis**
tent	**a tenda**
tent peg	**a estaca**
terrace	**a esplanada**
than: *better than*	*melhor do que*
thank you	**obrigado(a)**
thank you very much	*muito obrigado(a)*
that	**aquele (aquela)**
that one	**esse (essa)**
theatre	**o teatro**
then	**então**
there	**ali**
there is/there are	*há*
thermometer	**o termómetro**
these	**estes (estas)**
they	**eles (elas)** *see* GRAMMAR
thick	**grosso(a)**
thief	**o ladrão**
thigh	**a coxa**
thin	**magro(a)**
thing	**a coisa**
my things	*as minhas coisas*
think	**pensar**
third	**terceiro(a)**
thirsty: *I'm thirsty*	*tenho sede*
this	**este (esta)**
those	**aqueles (aquelas)**
thread	**a linha**
throat	**a garganta**
throat lozenges	**as pastilhas para a garganta**
through	**através de**
thunder	**o trovão**

ticket | **o bilhete**
ticket collector | **o revisor**
ticket office | **a bilheteira**
tide | **a maré**
tie | **a gravata**
tight | **apertado(a)**
tights | **os collants**
till *n* | **a caixa**
till *conj* | **até**
time | **o tempo**
what time is it? | *que horas são?*
this time | *esta vez*
timetable | **o horário**
tin | **a lata**
tinfoil | **a folha de estanho**
tin-opener | **o abre-latas**
tip | **a gorjeta**
tired | **cansado(a)**
tissue | **o lenço de papel**
to | **a**
to London | *para Londres*
to Spain | *para Espanha*
toast | **a torrada**
tobacconist's | **a tabacaria**
today | **hoje**
together | **juntos**
toilet | **a casa de banho**
toilet paper | **o papel higiénico**
toll | **a portagem**
tomato | **o tomate**
tomato juice | **o sumo de tomate**
tomorrow | **amanhã**
tongue | **a língua**
tonic water | **a água tónica**

tonight	**esta noite**
tooth	**o dente**
toothache	**a dor de dentes**
toothbrush	**a escova de dentes**
toothpaste	**a pasta dentífrica**
top *adj* **:** ***the top floor***	***o último andar***
top *n*	**a parte de cima**
on top of ...	***em cima de...***
torch	**a lanterna**
torn	**rasgado(a)**
total	**o total**
tough	**duro(a)**
tour	**a excursão**
tourist	**o/a turista**
tourist office	**o turismo**
tourist ticket	**o bilhete turístico**
tow	**rebocar**
towel	**o toalha**
tower	**a torre**
town	**a cidade**
town centre	**o centro da cidade**
town hall	**a Câmara Municipal**
town plan	**o mapa da cidade**
towrope	**o cabo de reboque**
toy	**o brinquedo**
traditional	**tradicional**
traffic	**o trânsito**
traffic lights	**o semáforo**
train	**o comboio**
tram	**o eléctrico**
translate	**traduzir**
translation	**a tradução**
travel	**viajar**

travel agent	**o agente de viagens**
traveller's cheques	**o cheque de viagem**
tray	**o tabuleiro ; a bandeja**
tree	**a árvore**
trip	**a viagem**
trouble	**os problemas**
trousers	**as calças**
trout	**a truta**
truck	**o camião**
true	**verdadeiro(a)**
trunks *(swimming)*	**os calções de banho**
truth	**a verdade**
try	**tentar**
try on *(clothes, shoes)*	**provar**
T-shirt	**a T-shirt**
tuna	**o atum**
tunnel	**o túnel**
turkey	**o perú**
turn	**voltar ; girar**
turn off	**apagar ; fechar ; desligar**
turn on	**acender ; abrir ; ligar**
tweezers	**a pinça**
twice	**duas vezes**
twin-bedded room	**o quarto com duas camas**
tyre	**o pneu**
tyre pressure	*a pressão dos pneus*
ugly	**feio(a)**
umbrella	**o guarda-chuva**
uncle	**o tio**
uncomfortable	**incómodo(a)**
unconscious	**inconsciente**

under	**debaixo de**
underground	**o metropolitano**
underpants	**as cuecas**
understand	**compreender**
I don't understand	*não compreendo*
underwear	**a roupa interior**
undo	**desfazer**
unemployed	**desempregado(a)**
unfasten	**desapertar ; desabotoar**
unleaded petrol	**a gasolina sem chumbo**
unhappy with...	**não estar satisfeito(a) com...**
United States	**os Estados Unidos**
university	**a universidade**
unlucky	**infeliz**
unpack *(suitcases)*	**desfazer as malas**
unscrew	**desaparafusar**
up *(out of bed)*	**levantado(a)**
upstairs	**em cima**
urgent	**urgente**
use	**utilizar**
useful	**útil**
usual	**habitual**
usually	**geralmente**

vacancies	**os quartos vagos**
vacuum cleaner	**o aspirador**
valid	**válido(a)**
valley	**o vale**
valuable	**valioso(a)**
valuables	**os objectos de valor**
van	**a carrinha**
vase *(for flowers)*	**a jarra**

VAT	o IVA
veal	a carne de vitela
vegetables *(cooked)*	os legumes
vegetarian	vegetariano(a)
vehicle	o veículo
vein	a veia
velvet	o veludo
ventilator	o ventilador
very	muito
vest	a camisola interior
video	o vídeo
video camera	a câmara de video
video recorder	o gravador de video
view	a vista
village	a aldeia
vinegar	o vinagre
vineyard	a vinha
visa	o visto
visit	visitar
vitamin	a vitamina
voice	a voz
volleyball	o voleibol
voltage	a voltagem

wage	o salário
waist	a cintura
wait (for)	esperar (por)
waiter	o empregado de mesa
waiting room	a sala de espera
waitress	a empregada de mesa
wake up	acordar
Wales	o País de Gales

walk *vb*	**andar**
walk *n*	**o passeio**
walking stick	**a bengala**
wall	**a parede**
wallet	**a carteira**
walnut	**a noz**
want	**querer**
war	**a guerra**
wardrobe	**o guarda-fato**
warm	**quente**
warning triangle	**o triângulo de sinalização**
wash	**lavar**
wash oneself	*lavar-se*
washbasin	**o lavatório**
washing machine	**a máquina de lavar roupa**
washing powder	**o detergente para a roupa**
washing-up liquid	**o detergente para a louça**
wasp	**a vespa**
waste bin	**o balde do lixo**
watch *n*	**o relógio**
watch *vb*	**ver**
watchstrap	**a pulseira de relógio**
water	**a água**
fresh water	*a água corrente*
salt water	*a água salgada*
waterfall	**a queda de água**
water heater	**o esquentador**
watermelon	**a melancia**
waterproof	**impermeável**
water-skiing	**o esqui aquático**
wave	**a onda**
wax	**a cera**
way	**a maneira ; o caminho**
we	**nós** see **GRAMMAR**

weak	**fraco(a)**
(tea, etc)	**aguado(a)**
wear	**vestir**
weather	**o tempo**
wedding	**o casamento**
week	**a semana**
weekday	**o dia útil**
weekend	**o fim-de-semana**
weekly	**por semana**
weight	**o peso**
welcome	**bem-vindo(a)**
well	**bem**
he's not well	***ele não se sente bem***
Welsh	**galês (galesa)**
west	**o oeste**
wet	**molhado(a)**
wetsuit	**o fato de mergulhador**
what	**que**
what is it?	***o que é?***
wheel	**a roda**
wheelchair	**a cadeira de rodas**
when	**quando**
where	**onde**
which: ***which is it?***	***qual é?***
while	**enquanto**
in a while	***dentro de pouco***
white	**branco(a)**
who: ***who is it?***	***quem é?***
whole	**inteiro(a)**
wholemeal	**integral**
whose: ***whose is it?***	***de quem é?***
why	**porquê?**
wide	**largo(a)**
wife	**a mulher ; a esposa**

wind	**o vento**
windmill	**o moínho**
window	**a janela**
(shop)	**a montra**
windscreen	**o pára-brisas**
windsurfing	**o wind-surf**
windy: ***it's windy***	***está vento***
wine	**o vinho**
wine list	**a lista de vinhos**
winter	**o inverno**
with	**com**
without	**sem**
woman	**a mulher**
wood *(substance)*	**a madeira**
woods	**a floresta**
wool	**a lã**
word	**a palavra**
work	**trabalhar ; funcionar**
world	**o mundo**
worried	**preocupado(a)**
worse	**pior**
worth: ***it's worth...***	***vale...***
wrap (up)	**embrulhar**
wrapping paper	**o papel de embrulho**
write	**escrever**
writing paper	**o papel de carta**
wrong	**errado(a)**
x-ray	**a radiografia**

yacht	**o iate**
year	**o ano**
yellow	**amarelo(a)**
yes	**sim**
yesterday	**ontem**
yet: ***not yet***	***ainda não***
yoghurt	**o iogurte**
you	**você/tu/vocês/vós** *see* **GRAMMAR**
young	**novo(a)**
(person)	**o/a jovem**
youth hostel	**o albergue da juventude**
zero	**o zero**
zip	**o fecho éclair**
zone	**a zona**
zoo	**o jardim zoológico**

a	**to ; the** *(feminine)*
à	**to the**
abadia *f*	**abbey**
abaixo	**down ; below**
aberto(a)	**open**
aberto todo o ano	**open all year round**
abrande	**slow down**
abre-garrafas *m*	**bottle-opener**
abre-latas *m*	**tin-opener ; can-opener**
Abril *m*	**April**
abrir	**to open; to unlock** *(door)*
acabar	**to end ; to finish**
acampar	**to camp**
aceitar	**to accept**
acelerador *m*	**accelerator**
acender	**to switch/turn on** *(radio, etc)* **; to light** *(fire, cigarette)*
acenda as luzes	**switch on headlights ; switch on lights** *(home, etc)*
acepipes *mpl*	**titbits**
aceso(a)	**on** *(light, etc)*
acesso *m*	**access**
achar	**to think ; to find**
acha bem?	**do you think it's alright?**
acidente *m*	**accident**
acima	**above**
aço *m*	**steel**
aço inoxidável	**stainless steel**
açorda *f*	**bread porridge**
açorda à alentejana	**bread, coriander and egg soup**
acordo *m*	**agreement**
Açores *mpl*	**the Azores islands**
actual	**present(-day)**
actualizar	**to modernize ; to update**

açúcar *m*	**sugar**
adega *f*	**wine cellar**
adesivo *m*	**plaster** *(for cut)*
adeus	**goodbye**
adiantado(a)	**fast** *(watch, etc)* **; early** *(train, etc)*
adulto(a)	**adult**
advogado *m*	**lawyer**
aéreo(a): a linha aérea	**airline**
via aérea	**air mail**
aeroporto *m*	**airport**
agência *f*	**agency**
agência de viagens	**travel agents**
agente *m/f*	**agent**
agora	**now**
Agosto *m*	**August**
agradável	**pleasant**
agradecer	**to thank**
água *f*	**water**
água destilada	**distilled water**
água potável	**drinking water**
aguardente *f*	**spirit brandy**
agudo(a)	**sharp** *(pain)*
ajudar	**to help**
albergue *m*	**hostel**
albergue da juventude	**youth hostel**
alcoólico(a)	**alcoholic**
aldeia *f*	**small village**
alegre	**jolly**
Alemanha *f*	**Germany**
alérgico(a) a	**allergic to**
alface *f*	**lettuce**
alfaiate *m*	**tailor**
alfândega *f*	**customs**
alfinete *m*	**pin**

alforreca *f*	**jellyfish**
algodão *m*	**cotton**
algum(a)	**some ; any**
alguns (algumas)	**a few ; some**
mais alguma coisa?	**anything else?**
alho *m*	**garlic**
alhos-porros *mpl*	**leeks**
ali	**there**
alimentação *f*	**food**
alívio *m*	**relief**
almoço *m*	**lunch**
pequeno-almoço *m*	**breakfast**
almofada *f*	**pillow ; cushion**
alojamento *m*	**accommodation**
alpinismo *m*	**climbing**
alto!	**stop!**
alto(a)	**high ; tall ; loud**
a estação alta	**high season**
altura *f*	**height**
alugar	**to hire ; to rent**
aluga-se	**for hire ; to rent**
alugam-se quartos	**rooms to let**
aluguer *m*	**rental**
amanhã	**tomorrow**
amarelo(a)	**yellow**
amargo(a)	**bitter**
ambulância *f*	**ambulance**
amêijoa *f*	**clam ; cockle**
amêijoas à Bulhão Pato	**clams with coriander, olive oil and garlic**
ameixa *f*	**plum**
ameixa seca	**prune**
amêndoa *f*	**almond**
amêndoa amarga	**bitter almond liqueur**
amendoim *m*	**peanut**

amigo(a) *m/f*	**friend**
amora *f*	**blackberry ; mulberry**
amortecedor *m*	**shock absorber**
amostra *f*	**sample**
analgésico *m*	**painkiller**
ananás *m*	**pineapple**
anchovas *fpl*	**anchovies**
andar	**to walk**
andar *m*	**floor ; storey**
anel *m*	**ring**
anis *m*	**aniseed liqueur**
aniversário *m*	**anniversary ; birthday**
ano *m*	**year**
Ano Novo	**New Year**
antes de	**before**
antiguidades *fpl*	**antiques**
apagado(a)	**off** *(radio, etc)* **; out** *(light, etc)*
apagar	**to switch/turn off** *(light, etc)*
aparelho *m*	**gadget ; machine**
aparelho para a surdez	**hearing aid**
apartamento *m*	**apartment ; flat**
apelido *m*	**surname**
apelido de solteira	**maiden name**
apenas	**only**
apertado(a)	**tight**
apetite *m*	**appetite**
bom apetite!	**enjoy your meal!**
apólice de seguro *f*	**insurance certificate**
aquecedor *m*	**heater ; electric fire**
aquecimento *m*	**heating**
aqui	**here**
ar *m*	**air ; choke** *(car)*
ar condicionado	**air conditioning**
arder	**to burn**

areia *f*	**sand**
arenque *m*	**herring**
armário *m*	**cupboard ; closet**
armazém *m*	**warehouse**
grande armazém	**department store**
arrendar	**to let**
arroz *m*	**rice**
arroz doce	**sweet rice dessert**
artesanato *m*	**handicrafts**
artigo *m*	**item**
artigos de ménage	**household goods**
artigos de vime	**wickerwork**
árvore *f*	**tree**
ascensor *m*	**lift ; elevator**
assado(a)	**roast ; baked**
assinar	**to sign**
assinatura *f*	**signature**
assistência *f*	**audience ; assistance**
atacadores *mpl*	**laces**
até	**till ; until**
aterrar	**to land**
atrás	**behind**
atrasado(a)	**late** *(for appointment)*
atrasar	**to delay**
atravessar	**to cross**
atum *m*	**tuna ; tunny fish**
autocarro *m*	**bus ; coach**
a paragem de autocarro	**bus stop**
auto-estrada *f*	**motorway**
automobilista *m/f*	**driver**
automóvel *m*	**car**
autorização *f*	**licence ; permit**
avaria *f*	**breakdown**
avariado(a)	**broken down ; out of order**

ave *f*	**bird**
avelã *f*	**hazelnut**
avenida *f*	**avenue**
avião *m*	**plane**
aviso *m*	**warning**
avô *m*	**grandfather**
avó *f*	**grandmother**
azedo(a)	**sour**
azeite *m*	**olive oil**
azeitona *f*	**olive**
azul	**blue**
azulejo *m*	**ornamental tile**
bacalhau *m*	**salt cod**
bacalhau à Brás	**salt cod with eggs, onion and potatoes**
bagaceira *f*	**eau de vie**
bagaço *m*	**eau de vie**
bagagem *f*	**luggage ; baggage**
Bairrada	**region producing full-bodied red and aromatic white wines**
bairro *m*	**quarter ; district**
baixar	**to lower**
baixo: em baixo	**below**
balcão *m*	**counter** *(shop)* **; circle** *(theatre)*
banco *m*	**bank ; seat** *(in car, etc)***; casualty department** *(hospital)*
banheiro *m*	**lifeguard**
banho *m*	**bath**
a casa de banho	**bathroom ; toilet**
tomar banho	**to bathe ; to take a bath**
barato(a)	**cheap**
barba *f*	**beard**

barbeiro *m*	**barber**
barco *m*	**boat ; ship**
barco a remos	**rowing boat**
barco à vela	**sailing boat**
barraca *f*	**hut** *(shed)* **; beach hut**
barriga *f*	**tummy ; belly**
barro *m*	**clay pottery ; earthenware**
barulho *m*	**noise**
bastante	**enough**
batata *f*	**potato**
batatas fritas	**chips ; crisps**
bater	**to beat ; to knock**
bata à porta	**please knock** *(at door)*
bateria *f*	**battery** *(for car)*
batido de leite *m*	**milk shake**
baunilha *f*	**vanilla**
bebé *m*	**baby**
beber	**to drink**
bebida *f*	**drink**
beco *m*	**alley**
belo(a)	**beautiful**
bem	**well**
está bem	**OK**
bem passado	**well done** *(steak)*
bem-vindo(a)	**welcome**
bengaleiro *m*	**cloakroom** *(at theatre)*
beringela *f*	**aubergine**
berma *f*	**hard shoulder**
bermas baixas	**steep verge–no hard shoulder**
besugo *m*	**sea bream**
beterraba *f*	**beetroot**
bica *f*	**small strong black coffee**
bicha *f*	**queue**
fazer bicha	**to queue**
bicicleta *f*	**bicycle ; cycle**

bife *m*	**steak**
bife com batatas fritas	**steak and chips**
bifurcação *f*	**junction**
bilhar *m*	**billiards**
bilhete *m*	**ticket ; fare**
bilhete de entrada	**admission ticket**
bilhete de identidade	**identity card**
bilheteira *f*	**booking office ; ticket office**
binóculos *mpl*	**binoculars**
boa	*see* **bom**
boca *f*	**mouth**
bocado: um bocado	**a bit ; a portion**
boîte *f*	**nightclub**
bola *f*	**ball**
bola de Berlim	**doughnut**
bolacha *f*	**biscuit**
bolo *m*	**cake**
bolo-rei	**ring-shaped fruit cake eaten at Christmas**
bolsa *f*	**stock exchange ; handbag**
bom (boa)	**good ; fine** *(weather)* **; kind**
bom dia	**good morning**
boa noite	**good evening ; good night**
boa tarde	**good afternoon**
bomba *f*	**bomb ; pump** *(petrol)*
bombeiros *mpl*	**fire brigade**
boneco(a)	**doll ; puppet toy**
bonito(a)	**pretty**
borbulha *f*	**heat rash ; spots** *(on skin)*
bordados *mpl*	**embroidered items**
borrego *m*	**lamb**
bosque *m*	**forest ; woodland**
bota *f*	**boot** *(to wear)*
braço *m*	**arm**
branco(a)	**white**

brigada de trânsito *f*	**traffic police**
brincos *mpl*	**earrings**
brinquedo *m*	**toy**
britânico(a)	**British**
broa *f*	**corn (maize) bread**
broas	**corn (maize) cakes**
bronzeador *m*	**suntan oil**
brushing *m*	**blow-dry**
bugigangas *fpl*	**bric-à-brac**
buscar	**to seek**
bússola *f*	**compass**
buzinar	**to toot car horn**

cabeça *f*	**head**
cabedais *mpl*	**leather goods**
cabeleireiro *m*	**hairdresser**
cabelo *m*	**hair**
cabide *m*	**coat hanger ; peg** *(for clothes)*
cabine *f*	**berth** *(on boat)* **; booth**
cabine telefónica	**telephone box**
cabo *m*	**handle** *(of knife)* **; lead** *(electric)*
cabos de emergência	**jump leads**
cabo de reboque	**tow rope**
cabrito *m*	**kid goat**
caça *f*	**game** *(to eat)* **; hunting**
cachorro *m*	**hot dog ; puppy**
cada	**each ; every**
cadeado *m*	**padlock**
cadeira *f*	**chair**
cadeira de bebé	**high chair ; push chair**
cadeira de lona	**deck chair**
cadeira de rodas	**wheelchair**
café *m*	**(black) coffee ; café**

cair	**to fall ; to fall over**
cais *m*	**quay**
caixa *f*	**box** *(container)* **; cash desk ; till**
caixa automática	**cash machine**
caixa do correio	**letterbox**
caixote *m*	**bin**
calças *fpl*	**trousers**
calções *mpl*	**shorts**
calções de banho	**swimming trunks**
calços para travões *mpl*	**brake pads**
caldeirada *f*	**fish stew**
caldo *m*	**stock** *(for soup)*
caldo verde	**cabbage soup**
calor *m*	**heat**
calorífero *m*	**heater**
cama *f*	**bed**
cama de casal	**double bed**
cama de criança	**cot**
cama de pessoa só	**single bed**
a roupa de cama	**bedding**
câmara de ar *f*	**inner tube**
câmara municipal *f*	**town hall**
camarão *m*	**shrimp**
camarote *m*	**cabin**
cambiar	**to exchange; to change** *(money)*
câmbio *m*	**exchange rate**
camião *m*	**lorry**
caminho *m*	**track** *(path)* **; way ; route**
camioneta *f*	**coach**
camisa *f*	**shirt**
camisa de noite	**nightdress**
campaínha *f*	**bell** *(on door)*
campismo *m*	**camping**
campo *m*	**field ; countryside**

campo de golfe — **golf course**
camurça *f* — **suede**
cancelar — **to cancel**
canela *f* — **cinnamon**
caneta *f* — **pen**
cano de esgoto *m* — **drain**
canoagem *f* — **canoeing**
cansado(a) — **tired**
cantina *f* — **canteen**
canto *m* — **corner**
cão *m* — **dog**
capacete *m* — **crash helmet**
capela *f* — **chapel**
capot *m* — **bonnet** *(of car)*
cara *f* — **face**
caracóis *mpl* — **snails ; curls** *(hair)*
caramelos *mpl* — **toffees**
caranguejo *m* — **crab**
carapau *m* — **horse-mackerel**
caravana *f* — **caravan**
carburador *m* — **carburettor**
carga *f* — **refill ; load**
caril *m* — **curry**
carioca *m* — **weak coffee**
  carioca de limão — **lemon tea**
carne *f* — **meat**
  carne de borrego — **spring lamb**
  carne picada — **mince**
  carne de porco — **pork**
  carne de vaca — **beef**
  carne de vitela — **veal**
  carnes frias — **cold meats**
carneiro *m* — **mutton ; lamb**
caro(a) — **dear ; expensive**

churrascaria *f*	**barbecue restaurant**
churrasco *m*	**barbecue**
no churrasco	**barbecued**
chuva *f*	**rain**
chuveiro *m*	**shower** *(bath)*
Cia.	*see* **companhia**
cidadão (cidadã) *m/f*	**citizen**
cidade *f*	**town ; city**
cigarro *m*	**cigarette**
cima : em cima de	**on (top of)**
cinco	**five**
cinto *m*	**belt**
cinto de salvação	**lifebelt**
cinto de segurança	**seat belt**
cinzento(a)	**grey**
circuito *m*	**circuit**
circular *f*	**roundabout** *(for traffic)*
irurgia *f*	**surgery** *(operation)*
laro(a)	**light** *(colour)* **; bright**
lasse *f*	**class**
liente *m/f*	**client**
ínica *f*	**clinic**
ube *m*	**club**
bertor *m*	**blanket**
brador *m*	**collector** *(of money, bills, on bus)*
rar	**to cash**
rir	**to cover**
igo *m*	**code ; dialling code**
digo postal	**postcode**
rniz *f*	**quail**
o *m*	**rabbit**
tro *m*	**coriander**
m	**safe**
elo *m*	**mushroom**

carrinha *f*	**van**
carrinho *m*	**trolley**
carrinho de bebé	**pram ; carry cot**
carro *m*	**car**
carruagem *f*	**carriage** *(railway)*
carruagem-cama	**sleeper** *(railway)*
carruagem-restaurante *f*	**restaurant car**
carta *f*	**letter**
cartão *m*	**card ; business card**
cartão bancário	**cheque card**
cartão de crédito	**credit card**
cartão de embarque	**boarding card**
cartão de felicitações	**greetings card**
cartão garantia	**cheque card**
carteira *f*	**wallet**
carteirista *m*	**pickpocket**
carteiro *m*	**postman**
carvão *m*	**coal**
casa *f*	**home ; house**
casa de banho	**toilet ; bathroom**
casa de jantar	**dining room**
casaco *m*	**jacket ; coat**
casado(a)	**married**
casal *m*	**couple**
casamento *m*	**wedding**
caso *m*	**case**
em caso de...	**in case of...**
castanha *f*	**chestnut**
castanhas assadas	**roast chestnuts**
castanhas piladas	**dried chestnuts**
castanho(a)	**brown**
castelo *m*	**castle**
catedral *f*	**cathedral**
causa *f*	**cause**
por causa de	**because**

Portuguese	English
cautela	**take care**
cavala *f*	**mackerel**
cavalheiro *m*	**gentleman**
cavalheiros	**Gentlemen ; Gents'**
cavalo *m*	**horse**
cave (c/v) *f*	**cellar ; basement**
cebola *f*	**onion**
cedo	**early**
cego(a) *m/f*	**blind** *(person)*
ceia *f*	**supper**
célebre	**famous**
cem	**one hundred**
cemitério *m*	**cemetery**
cenoura *f*	**carrot**
centígrado *m*	**centigrade**
centímetro *m*	**centimetre**
cento: por cento	**per cent**
centro *m*	**centre**
centro da cidade	**city/town centre**
centro comercial	**shopping centre**
centro de saúde	**health centre**
cera *f*	**wax**
cerâmica *f*	**pottery**
cérebro *m*	**brain**
cereja *f*	**cherry**
certeza *f*	**certainty**
ter a certeza	**to be sure**
certificado *m*	**certificate**
certo(a)	**right** *(correct, accurate)* **; certain**
cerveja *f*	**beer ; lager**
cerveja preta	**bitter** *(beer)*
cervejaria *f*	**beer house**
cesto *m*	**basket**
céu *m*	**sky**

Portuguese	English
chá *f*	**tea**
chá de limão	**lemon tea**
chamada *f*	**telephone call**
chamada gratuita	**free call**
chamada internacional	**international call**
chamada pagável no destino	**reverse charge call**
chamar	**to call**
champô *m*	**shampoo**
chão *m*	**floor**
chapa de matrícula *f*	**number plate** *(on car)*
chapéu *m*	**hat**
chapéu de sol	**sunhat**
charcutaria *f*	**delicatessen**
chave *f*	**key**
fechar à chave	**to lock up**
chávena *f*	**cup**
chefe *m*	**boss**
chefe de cozinha	**chef**
chega!	**that's enough!**
chegadas *fpl*	**arrivals**
chegar	**to arrive**
cheio(a)	**full**
cheirar	**to smell**
cheiro *m*	**smell**
mau cheiro	**bad smell**
cheque *m*	**cheque**
cheque de viagem	**traveller'**
levantar um cheque	**to cash a**
cherne *m*	**black je**
chispalhada *f*	**bean s**
chispe *m*	**pig's t**
chocos *mpl*	**cuttle**
chocos com tinta	**cuttl**
chouriço *m*	**spic**

coisa *f*	**thing**
cola *f*	**glue**
colar *n*	**necklace**
colar *vb*	**to stick**
colcha *f*	**bedspread**
colchão *m*	**mattress**
colecção *f*	**collection** *(of stamps etc)*
colégio *m*	**school**
colete de salvação *m*	**life jacket**
colher *f*	**spoon**
colina *f*	**hill**
collants *mpl*	**tights**
colorau *m*	**paprika**
coluna *f*	**pillar**
coluna vertebral	**spine**
com	**with**
comandos *mpl*	**controls**
comboio *m*	**train**
combustível *m*	**fuel**
começar	**to begin ; to start**
comer	**to eat**
comida *f*	**food**
comissário de bordo *m*	**steward ; purser**
como	**as ; how**
como disse?	**I beg your pardon?**
como está?	**how are you?**
comodidade *f*	**comfort**
companhia (Cia.) *f*	**company**
compartimento *m*	**compartment**
completar	**to complete**
completo(a)	**full ; no vacancies**
compota *f*	**jam**
compra *f*	**purchase**
ir às compras	**to go shopping**

comprar	**to buy**
compreender	**to understand**
comprido(a)	**long**
comprimento *m*	**length**
comprimido *m*	**pill ; tablet ; squeezed**
computador *m*	**computer**
concelho *m*	**council**
concordar	**to agree**
concorrente *m/f*	**candidate**
concurso *m*	**competition**
condução *f*	**driving**
a carta de condução	**driving licence**
condutor *m*	**driver ; chauffeur**
conduzir	**to drive**
conferência *f*	**conference**
conferir	**to check**
congelado(a)	**frozen** *(food)*
congelar	**to freeze**
não congelar	**do not freeze**
conhaque *m*	**cognac**
conhecer	**to know** *(person, place)*
conselho *m*	**advice**
consertos *mpl*	**repairs**
conservar	**to keep ; to preserve**
conservar no frio	**store in a cold place**
constipação *f*	**cold** *(illness)*
consulado *m*	**consulate**
consulta *f*	**consultation ; appointment**
consultório *m*	**surgery**
consumir antes de ...	**best before ...** *(label on food)*
conta *f*	**account; bill**
contador *m*	**meter** *(electricity, water)*
conter	**to contain**
não contem ...	**does not contain ...**

conto *m*	**= 1000 escudos**
contra	**against**
contraceptivo *m*	**contraceptive**
contrato *m*	**contract**
convidado(a) *m/f*	**guest**
convidar	**to invite ; to ask** *(invite)*
convite *m*	**invitation**
copo *m*	**glass** *(container)*
cor *f*	**colour**
coração *m*	**heart**
cordeiro *m*	**lamb**
cor de laranja	**orange** *(colour)*
cor-de-rosa	**pink**
corpo *m*	**body**
correia *f*	**strap**
correia de ventoinha	**fan belt**
correio *m*	**post office**
pelo correio	**by post**
corrente *f*	**chain ; current**
correr	**to flow ; to run** *(person)*
correspondência *f*	**mail**
corrida *f*	**bullfight**
corridas de cavalos	**races**
cortar	**to cut ; to cut off**
cortar e fazer brushing	**cut and blow-dry**
corte *m*	**cut**
cortiça *f*	**cork**
costa *f*	**shore ; coastline**
costela *f*	**rib**
costeleta *f*	**chop** *(meat)* **; cutlet**
cotovelo *m*	**elbow**
couro *m*	**leather**
couve *f*	**cabbage**
couves de Bruxelas	**Brussels sprouts**

couve-flor *f*	**cauliflower**
coxia *f*	**aisle**
cozer	**to boil**
cozido(a)	**boiled**
mal cozido	**underdone**
cozinha *f*	**kitchen**
cozinhar	**to cook**
cozinheiro(a) *m/f*	**cook**
cravinhos *mpl*	**cloves**
cravo *m*	**carnation**
creme *f*	**custard ; foundation cream**
creme de barbear	**shaving cream**
creme para bronzear	**suntan cream**
creme hidratante	**moisturizer**
creme de limpeza	**cleansing cream**
criança *f*	**child**
cru(a)	**raw**
cruz *f*	**cross**
cruzamento *m*	**junction** *(crossroads)*
cruzar	**to cross**
cruzeiro *m*	**cruise**
cuecas *fpl*	**briefs ; pants**
cuidado *m*	**care** *(caution)*
cumprimento *m*	**greeting**
cumprimentos	**regards**
curso *m*	**course**
curto(a)	**short**
curva *f*	**bend ; turning ; curve**
curva perigosa	**dangerous bend**
custar	**to cost**
custo *m*	**charge ; cost**
c/v	*see* **cave**

damasco *m*	**apricot**
dança *f*	**dance**
dano *m*	**damage**
Dão	**fruity red and white wines from the north of Portugal**
dar	**to give**
dar prioridade	**to give way**
data *f*	**date**
data de nascimento	**date of birth**
de	**of ; from**
debaixo de	**under**
decidir	**to decide**
dedo *m*	**finger**
dedo do pé	**toe**
defeito *m*	**flaw**
deficiente	**disabled ; handicapped**
degrau *m*	**step** *(stair)*
deitar-se	**to lie down**
deixar	**to let** *(allow)* **; to leave behind**
delito *m*	**crime**
demais	**too much ; too many**
demasia *f*	**change** *(money)* **; excess**
demorado(a)	**late**
demorar	**to delay**
dente *m*	**tooth**
dentes	**teeth**
dentes postiços	**false teeth**
dentista *m*	**dentist**
dentro	**inside**
depois	**after(wards)**
depósito *m*	**deposit** *(in bank)*
depósito de bagagens	**left-luggage (office)**
o depósito da gasolina	**petrol tank**
depressa	**quickly**

desafio *m*	**match ; game** *(sport)* **; challenge**
desaparecido(a)	**missing**
desapertar	**to loosen**
descafeinado *m*	**decaffeinated** *(tea, coffee)*
descansar	**to rest**
descartável	**throw-away ; disposable**
descer	**to go down**
descoberta *f*	**discovery**
descongelar	**to defrost** *(food)* **; to de-ice**
desconhecido(a) *m/f*	**stranger**
desconhecido(a) *adj*	**unknown**
desconto *m*	**discount ; reduction**
desculpe	**excuse me ; sorry** *(apology)*
desejar	**to desire ; to wish**
desembarcar	**to disembark**
desempregado(a)	**unemployed**
desenho *m*	**design** *(pattern)* **; drawing**
desinchar	**to go down** *(swelling)*
desinfectante *m*	**disinfectant**
desligado(a)	**off** *(engine, gas)*
desligar	**to hang up** *(phone)* **; to switch off** *(engine, radio)*
desligue o motor	**switch off your motor**
desmaiar	**to faint**
desodorizante *m*	**deodorant**
despachante *m*	**shipper ; transport agent**
despesa *f*	**expense**
desporto *m*	**sport**
destinatário *m*	**addressee**
desvio *m*	**bypass ; detour ; diversion**
detergente *m*	**detergent**
detergente para a louça	**washing-up liquid**
detergente para a roupa	**washing powder**

devagar	**slowly ; slow down** *(sign)*
dever: eu devo	**I must**
deve-me ...	**you owe me ...**
devolver	**to give back ; to return**
Dezembro *m*	**December**
dia *m*	**day**
dia útil	**working day**
dias da semana	**weekdays**
dia de anos	**birthday**
diabético(a)	**diabetic**
diante de	**in front of** *(place)*
diário	**daily**
diarreia *f*	**diarrhoea**
dieta *f*	**diet ; special regime**
diferença *f*	**difference**
difícil	**difficult**
digestão *f*	**digestion**
diluir	**to dilute**
diminuir	**to reduce**
dínamo *m*	**dynamo**
dinheiro *m*	**money ; cash**
direcção *f*	**direction ; address ; steering**
directo(a)	**direct**
direita *f*	**right(-hand side)**
à direita	**on the right**
para a direita	**to the right**
direito(a)	**straight ; right(-hand)**
Dto.	**on right-hand side** *(address)*
direitos *mpl*	**duty** *(tax)* **; rights**
dirigir	**to direct**
disco *m*	**record** *(music, etc)*
disco de estacionamento	**parking disk**
disponível	**available**
dissolver	**to dissolve**

distância *f*	**distance**
distrito *m*	**district**
divã-cama *m*	**bed-settee**
diversões *fpl*	**entertainment**
divertir-se	**to enjoy oneself ; to have fun**
dívida *f*	**debt**
divisas *fpl*	**foreign currency**
dizer	**to say**
dobrada *f*	**tripe**
dobrado(a)	**bent**
dobro *m*	**double**
doce *adj*	**sweet** *(taste)*
doce *m*	**dessert**
documentos *mpl*	**documents**
doente	**ill ; sick**
doer	**to ache ; to hurt**
dólar *m*	**dollar**
domicílio *m*	**residence**
domingo *m*	**Sunday**
dono(a) *m/f*	**owner**
dona de casa	**housewife**
dor *f*	**ache ; pain**
dormir	**to sleep**
Douro	**region producing port wine**
Dto.	*see* **direito(a)**
duche *m*	**shower**
duplo(a)	**double**
durante	**during**
durar	**to last**
duro(a)	**hard ; stiff ; tough** *(meat)*
dúzia *f*	**dozen**

e	**and**
é	**he/she/it is ; you are**
economizar	**to save**
écrã *m*	**screen**
edifício *m*	**building**
edredão *m*	**duvet ; quilt**
educado(a)	**polite**
eixo de roda *m*	**axle**
ela	**she ; her ; it**
elástico *m*	**rubber band ; elastic band**
ele	**he ; him ; it**
eles	**they** *(masculine)*
electricista *m*	**electrician**
eléctrico *m*	**tram**
electrodomésticos *mpl*	**electrical appliances**
elevador *m*	**lift**
em	**at ; in** *(with towns, countries)* **; into**
embaixada *f*	**embassy**
embarcar	**to board** *(ship, plane)*
embarque *m*	**embarkation ; time of sailing**
embraiagem *f*	**clutch**
ementa *f*	**menu**
emergência *f*	**emergency**
empregado(a) *m/f*	**waiter(ess) ; maid ; attendant** *(at petrol station)* **; assistant** *(in shop)* **; employee** *(in office)*
emprego *m*	**job ; employment**
empurrar	**to push**
empurre	**push** *(sign on door)*
EN	*see* **estrada**
encaracolado(a)	**curly**
encarnado(a)	**red**
encerrado(a)	**closed**
encher	**to fill up ; to pump up** *(tyre, etc)*

enchidos *mpl*	**processed meats ; sausages**
encomenda *f*	**parcel**
encontrar	**to meet ; to find**
encontro *m*	**date ; meeting**
encosta *f*	**hill** *(slope)*
endereço *m*	**address**
energia *f*	**energy**
o corte de energia	**power cut**
enfermeiro(a) *m/f*	**nurse**
enganar-se	**to make a mistake**
engano *m*	**mistake**
engolir	**to swallow**
não engolir	**do not swallow**
engraxar	**to polish** *(shoes)*
enguia *f*	**eel**
enjoar	**to be sick**
ensinar	**to teach**
ensopado *m*	**stew served on slice of bread**
enorme	**big ; huge**
entender	**to understand**
entorse *f*	**sprain**
entrada *f*	**entrance ; starter** *(in meal)*
entrada livre	**admission free**
entrar	**to go in ; to come in ; to get into** *(car, etc)*
entre	**among ; between**
entregar	**to deliver**
entrevista *f*	**interview**
enviar	**to send**
enxaqueca *f*	**migraine**
época *f*	**period**
equipamento *m*	**equipment**
equitação *f*	**horse riding**
erro *m*	**mistake**

erva *f*	**grass ; herb**
ervilhas *fpl*	**peas**
esc.	*see* **escudo**
escada *f*	**ladder ; stairs**
escada rolante	**escalator**
escalfado(a)	**poached** *(egg)*
escape *m*	**exhaust**
escocês (escocesa)	**Scottish**
Escócia *f*	**Scotland**
escola *f*	**school**
escova *f*	**brush**
escova de dentes	**toothbrush**
escrever	**to write**
escrito: por escrito	**in writing**
escritório *m*	**office**
escudo (esc.) *m*	**escudo** *(Portuguese currency)*
escuro(a)	**dark** *(colour)*
escutar	**to listen to**
esferográfica *f*	**ballpoint pen**
esgotado(a)	**sold out** *(tickets)* **; exhausted**
esgoto *m*	**drain**
esmalte *m*	**enamel**
espaço *m*	**space**
espadarte *m*	**swordfish**
espalhar	**to scatter**
Espanha *f*	**Spain**
espanhol(a)	**Spanish**
espargo *m*	**asparagus**
esparguete *m*	**spaghetti**
esparregado *m*	**puréed spinach**
especialidade *f*	**speciality**
especiarias *fpl*	**spices**
espectáculo *m*	**show** *(in theatre etc)*

espelho *m*	**mirror**
espelho retrovisor	**driving mirror**
esperar	**to expect ; to hope**
esperar por	**to wait for**
espetada *f*	**kebab**
espinafre *m*	**spinach**
esplanada *f*	**terrace**
esposa *f*	**wife**
espumante *m*	**sparkling wine**
espumoso(a)	**sparkling** *(wine)*
Esq.	*see* **esquerda**
esquadra *f*	**police station**
esquentador *m*	**water heater**
esquerda *f*	**left(-hand side)**
à esquerda	**on the left**
Esq.	**on left(-hand) side** *(address)*
esqui *m*	**ski**
esquina *f*	**corner** *(outside)*
está	**he/she/it is ; you are**
estação *f*	**station**
estação alta	**high season**
estação do ano	**season**
estação baixa	**low season**
estação do comboio	**railway station**
estação de serviço	**service station**
estacionamento *m*	**parking**
estacionar	**to park** *(car)*
estádio *m*	**stadium**
estado *m*	**state**
estado civil	**marital status**
Estados Unidos (EUA) *mpl*	**United States**
estalagem *f*	**inn**
estância termal *f*	**spa**
estar	**to be**

este/esta *m/f*	**this**
estes/estas *m/f*	**these**
estômago *m*	**stomach**
o mal-estar de estômago	**stomach upset**
estores *mpl*	**blinds**
estrada *f*	**road**
estrada em mau estado	**uneven road surface**
estrada nacional (EN)	**major road ; national highway**
estrada sem saída	**no through road**
estrada secundária	**minor road**
estrangeiro(a) *m/f*	**foreigner**
estranho(a)	**strange**
estreito(a)	**narrow**
estudante *m/f*	**student**
estufado(a)	**braised**
etiqueta *f*	**ticket ; label ; etiquette**
eu	**I**
EUA	*see* **Estados Unidos**
europeu (europeia)	**European**
evitar	**to avoid**
excepto	**except**
excepto aos domingos	**Sundays excepted**
excesso de bagagem *m*	**excess luggage**
excursão *f*	**excursion ; tour**
excursão guiada	**guided tour**
exemplo *m*	**example**
por exemplo	**for example**
expirar	**to expire**
explicar	**to explain**
exportação *f*	**exportation**
exportar	**to export**
exposição *f*	**exhibition**
extintor *m*	**fire extinguisher**
extremidade *f*	**edge ; extremity**

fábrica *f* **factory**
fabricado(a) em ... **made in ...**
faca *f* **knife**
fácil **easy**
facilidade *f* **facility ; ease**
factura *f* **invoice**
fado *m* **traditional Portuguese song**
faiança *f* **pottery**
faisão *m* **pheasant**
faixa *f* **lane** *(in road)*
falar **to speak**
falecido(a) **deceased**
falésias *fpl* **cliffs**
falta *f* **lack**
  falta de corrente **power cut**
família *f* **family**
farinha *f* **flour**
farinheira *f* **sausage made with pork fat and flour**
farmácia *f* **chemist's**
  farmácia permanente **duty chemist**
  farmácias de serviço **emergency chemists'**
faróis *mpl* **headlights**
farol *m* **headlight ; lighthouse**
farolim *m* **sidelight**
fatia *f* **slice**
fato *m* **suit** *(man's)*
  fato de banho **swimsuit**
  fato de treino **track suit**
favas *fpl* **broad beans**
favor *m* **favour**
  por favor **please**
  faz favor **please**
fazer **to do ; to make**
febras de porco *fpl* **thin slices of roast pork**

febre *f*	**fever**
febre dos fenos	**hay fever**
fechado(a)	**shut ; closed**
fechado para férias	**closed for holidays**
fechar	**to shut ; to close**
feijão *m*	**beans**
feijão-verde *m*	**French beans**
feijoada *f*	**bean stew with pork and spicy sausage**
feio(a)	**awful ; ugly**
feira *f*	**fair** *(commercial)* **; market**
feito(a) à mão	**handmade**
feliz	**happy**
feriado *m*	**public holiday**
feriado nacional	**bank holiday**
férias *fpl*	**holidays**
ferido(a)	**injured**
ferragens *fpl*	**ironware**
ferro *m*	**iron**
ferro de engomar	**iron** *(for clothes)*
ferver	**to boil**
festa *f*	**party** *(celebration)*
Fevereiro *m*	**February**
fiambre *m*	**ham**
ficar	**to stay ; to be ; to remain**
ficar bem	**to suit**
ficha *f*	**plug** *(electrical)* **; registration card** *(in hotel, clinic)*
ficha dupla/tripla	**adaptor** *(electrical)*
fígado *m*	**liver**
figo *m*	**fig**
figos secos	**dried figs**
fila *f*	**row** *(line)* **; queue**
filete *m*	**fillet steak ; tenderloin**
filha *f*	**daughter**

filho *m*	**son**
filial *f*	**branch** *(of bank, etc)*
filigranas *fpl*	**filigree work**
fim *m*	**end**
fim-de-semana	**weekend**
fio *m*	**wire**
fita *f*	**tape ; ribbon**
fita métrica	**tape measure**
flor *f*	**flower**
floresta *f*	**forest**
florista *f*	**florist**
fogão *m*	**cooker**
fogo *m*	**fire**
fogo de artifício	**fireworks**
folha *f*	**leaf**
folha de alumínio	**foil** *(for cooking)*
folha de estanho	**tinfoil**
folhados *mpl*	**puff pastries**
folheto *m*	**leaflet**
fome *f*	**hunger**
tenho fome	**I'm hungry**
fonte *f*	**fountain ; source**
fora	**out ; outside**
força *f*	**power** *(strength)* **; force**
formiga *f*	**ant**
fornecer	**to supply**
forno *m*	**oven**
fortaleza *f*	**fortress**
forte	**strong**
forte *f*	**fortress**
fósforo *m*	**match**
fotografia *f*	**photograph ; print** *(photoh)*
fraco(a)	**weak**
fralda *f*	**nappy**

framboesa *f*	**raspberry**
França *f*	**France**
francês (francesa)	**French**
frango *m*	**chicken** *(young and tender)*
frase *f*	**sentence**
freguês (freguesa) *m/f*	**customer**
frente *f*	**front**
em frente de	**in front of ; opposite**
fresco(a)	**fresh ; cool ; crisp**
frigorífico *m*	**fridge**
frio(a)	**cold**
fritar	**to fry**
frito(a)	**fried**
fronha *f*	**pillow case**
fronteira *f*	**border** *(frontier)*
fruta *f*	**fruit**
frutaria *f*	**fruit shop**
fruto *m*	**fruit**
fuga *f*	**leak**
fumador(a) *m/f*	**smoker**
para não fumadores	**non-smoking** *(compartment, etc)*
fumar	**to smoke**
não fumar	**no smoking**
fumo *m*	**smoke**
funcionar	**to work** *(machine)*
não funciona	**out of order**
funcionário(a) *m/f*	**employee ; civil servant**
fundo *m*	**bottom**
fundo(a)	**deep**
furar	**to pierce**
furnas *fpl*	**caverns**
furto *m*	**theft**
fusível *m*	**fuse**
futebol *m*	**football**

gabinete de provas *m*	**changing room**
gado *m*	**cattle**
gado bravo	**beware – unfenced bulls**
gaivota *f*	**seagull ; pedal boat**
galão *m*	**large white coffee ; gallon**
galeria *f*	**gallery**
Gales : o País de Gales	**Wales**
galês (galesa)	**Welsh**
galinha *f*	**hen ; chicken**
gamba *f*	**prawn**
ganhar	**to earn ; to win**
ganso *m*	**goose**
garagem *f*	**garage**
garantia *f*	**guarantee**
gare *f*	**quay ; platform**
garfo *m*	**fork**
garganta *f*	**throat**
garoto *m*	**little boy ; small white coffee**
garrafa *f*	**bottle**
garrafão *m*	**two or five-litre bottle**
gás *m*	**gas**
a botija de gás	**gas cylinder**
gasóleo *m*	**diesel**
gasolina *f*	**petrol**
gasosa *f*	**fizzy sweetened water**
gastar	**to spend**
gaveta *f*	**drawer**
gelado *m*	**ice cream ; ice lolly**
gelar	**to freeze**
gelataria *f*	**ice cream parlour**
geleia *f*	**jelly**
gelo *m*	**ice**
gémeo(a)	**twin**

género *m*	**kind ; type**
gengibre *m*	**ginger**
gengivas *fpl*	**gums**
gente *f*	**people**
toda a gente	**everybody**
geral *f*	**gallery** *(in theatre)*
geral *adj*	**general**
em geral	**generally**
geralmente	**usually**
gerente *m*	**manager**
ginjinha *f*	**morello cherry liqueur**
gira-discos *m*	**record player**
girassol *m*	**sunflower**
gola *f*	**collar**
golfe *m*	**golf**
o taco de golfe	**golf club** *(stick)*
gordo(a)	**fat**
gorjeta *f*	**tip** *(to waiter, etc)*
gostar de	**to like**
gosto *m*	**taste**
governo *m*	**government**
Grã-Bretanha *f*	**Britain**
grama *m*	**gramme**
grande	**big ; large ; great**
grão *m*	**chickpeas**
grátis	**free** *(costing nothing)*
gravador *m*	**tape recorder**
gravata *f*	**tie**
grávida	**pregnant**
gravura *f*	**print** *(picture)*
grelhado(a)	**grilled**
greve *f*	**strike** *(industrial)*
em greve	**on strike**
gripe *f*	**flu**

groselha *f* — **(red)currant**
grosso(a) — **thick**
grupo *m* — **group ; party** *(group)*
  grupo sanguíneo — **blood group**
grutas *fpl* — **caves**
guarda *m/f* — **police officer**
guarda-chuva *m* — **umbrella**
guarda-lamas *m* — **mudguard**
guardanapo *m* — **napkin**
guardar — **to keep ; to watch over**
guarda-sol *m* — **sunshade**
guia *m/f* — **guide**
guiché *m* — **window** *(at post office, bank)*
guisado *m* — **stew**
guitarra *f* — **guitar**

há — **there is ; there are**
habitação *f* — **residence ; home**
habitar — **to reside**
história *f* — **history ; story**
hoje — **today**
homem *m* — **man**
homens *mpl* — **Gents'**
hora *f* — **hour ; time** *(by the clock)*
  hora de chegada — **time of arrival**
  hora de partida — **time of departure**
  hora de ponta — **rush hour**
horário *m* — **timetable**
hortelã *f* — **mint** *(herb)*
hortelã-pimenta *f* — **peppermint** *(herb)*
hóspede *m/f* — **guest**
hospedeira *f* — **hostess**
  hospedeira de bordo — **stewardess ; air hostess**

iate *m*	**yacht**
icterícia *f*	**jaundice**
ida *f*	**visit ; trip**
ida e volta	**return trip**
idade *f*	**age**
identificação *f*	**identification**
idosos *mpl*	**the elderly ; old people**
ignição *f*	**ignition ; starter** *(in car)*
igreja *f*	**church**
igual	**equal ; the same as**
ilha *f*	**island**
impedir	**to prevent**
impedido(a)	**engaged** *(phone)*
imperial *m*	**draught beer**
impermeável *m*	**raincoat ; waterproof**
importação *f*	**importation**
importância *f*	**importance ; amount** *(money)*
importante	**important**
imposto *m*	**tax ; duty**
impostos	**duty ; tax**
impressão digital *f*	**fingerprint**
impresso *m*	**form** *(to fill in)*
imprevisto(a)	**unexpected**
impulso *m*	**unit of charge** *(for phone)*
incêndio *m*	**fire**
inchado(a)	**swollen**
incluído(a)	**included**
incomodar	**to disturb**
não incomodar	**do not disturb**
indicativo *m*	**dialling code**
indigestão *f*	**indigestion**
infecção *f*	**infection**
infeccioso(a)	**infectious** *(illness)*
inflamação *f*	**inflammation**

informação *f*	**information**
infracção *f*	**offence**
Inglaterra *f*	**England**
inglês (inglesa)	**English**
iniciais *fpl*	**initials**
iniciar	**to begin**
início *m*	**beginning**
inquilino *m*	**tenant**
inscrever	**to register**
insecto *m*	**insect**
insolação *f*	**heatstroke ; sunstroke**
instalações *fpl*	**facilities**
instituto *m*	**institute**
insuflável	**inflatable**
inteiro(a)	**whole**
interdito(a)	**forbidden**
interessante	**interesting**
interior	**inside**
interno(a)	**internal**
intérprete *m/f*	**interpreter**
interruptor *m*	**switch**
intervalo *m*	**interval** *(in theatre)*
intestinos *mpl*	**bowels**
intoxicação *f*	**food poisoning**
introduzir	**to introduce**
inundação *f*	**flood**
inverno *m*	**winter**
iogurte *m*	**yoghurt**
ir	**to go**
Irlanda *f*	**Ireland**
a Irlanda do Norte	**Northern Ireland**
irlandês (irlandesa)	**Irish**
irmã *f*	**sister**

irmão *m* — **brother**
iscas *fpl* — **marinated pig's liver with potatoes**
isqueiro *m* — **lighter**
isso — **that**
isto — **this**
Itália *f* — **Italy**
italiano(a) — **Italian**
itinerário *m* — **route ; itinerary**
IVA *m* — **VAT**

já — **already ; now**
Janeiro *m* — **January**
janela *f* — **window**
jantar *m* — **dinner ; evening meal**
jardim *m* — **garden**
joalharia *f* — **jeweller's ; jewellery**
joelho *m* — **knee**
jogar — **to play**
jogo *m* — **match ; game; play**
jóia *f* — **jewel**
jornal *m* — **newspaper**
jovem — **young**
Julho *m* — **July**
Junho *m* — **June**
juntar — **to join**
junto — **near**
juventude *f* — **youth**

kg. — *see* **quilo(grama)**

lã *f*	**wool**
lábio *m*	**lip**
laço *m*	**bow** *(ribbon, string)*
lado *m*	**side**
ao lado de	**next to**
ladrão *m*	**thief**
lagarto *m*	**lizard**
lago *m*	**lake**
lagosta *f*	**lobster**
lagostim *m*	**king prawn**
lâminas de barbear *fpl*	**razor blades**
lâmpada *f*	**light bulb**
lampreia *f*	**lamprey eel**
lançar	**to throw**
lanchar	**to go for snack/light lunch**
lanche *m*	**light afternoon meal ; snack**
lápis *m*	**pencil**
lápis de cera	**crayons** *(wax)*
lar *m*	**home**
laranja *f*	**orange**
o doce de laranja	**marmalade**
largo *m*	**small square**
largo(a)	**broad ; loose** *(clothes)* **; wide**
largura *f*	**width**
lata *f*	**tin ; can** *(of food)*
latão *m*	**brass**
lavabo *m*	**lavatory ; toilet**
lava-louça *m*	**sink**
lavandaria *f*	**laundry**
lavandaria automática	**launderette**
lavandaria a seco	**dry-cleaner's**
lavar	**to wash** *(clothes, etc)*
lavar a louça	**to wash up**
lavar à mão	**to handwash**

lavável	**washable**
lebre *f*	**hare**
legumes *mpl*	**vegetables**
lei *f*	**law**
leilão *m*	**auction**
leitão *m*	**sucking pig**
leite *m*	**milk**
com leite	**white** *(coffee)*
leite desnatado	**skimmed milk**
leite evaporado	**evaporated milk**
leite gordo	**full cream milk**
leite de limpeza	**cleansing milk**
leite magro/meio gordo	**skimmed/semi-skimmed milk**
lembranças *fpl*	**souvenirs**
lembrar-se	**to remember**
leme *m*	**rudder ; helm**
lenço *m*	**handkerchief ; tissue**
lençol *m*	**sheet**
lente *f*	**lens**
lentes de contacto	**contact lenses**
lento(a)	**slow**
leque *m*	**fan** *(hand-held)*
ler	**to read**
leste *m*	**east**
letra *f*	**letter** *(of alphabet)*
letra maiúscula	**capital letter**
levantar	**to draw** *(money)* **; to lift**
levantar-se	**to stand up ; get up** *(from bed)*
levar	**to take ; to carry**
leve	**light** *(not heavy)*
libra *f*	**pound**
libras esterlinas	**pounds sterling**
lição *f*	**lesson**
licença *f*	**permit**
liceu *m*	**secondary school**

licor *m*	**liqueur**
ligação *f*	**connection** *(trains, etc)*
ligado(a)	**on** *(engine, gas, etc)*
ligeiro(a)	**light**
lima *f*	**lime** *(fruit)*
lima *f*	**file**
lima das unhas	**nailfile**
limão *m*	**lemon**
limite *m*	**limit**
limite de velocidade	**speed limit**
limonada *f*	**lemonade**
limpar	**to wipe ; to clean**
limpeza *f*	**cleaning**
limpeza a seco	**dry-cleaning**
limpo(a)	**clean**
língua *f*	**language ; tongue**
linguado *m*	**sole** *(fish)*
linguiça *f*	**narrow spicy pork sausage**
linha *f*	**line ; thread ; platform** *(railway)*
linho *m*	**linen**
liquidação *f*	**(clearance) sale**
Lisboa (Lx)	**Lisbon**
liso(a)	**smooth ; straight**
lista *f*	**list**
lista de preços	**price list**
lista telefónica	**telephone directory**
litro *m*	**litre**
livraria *f*	**bookshop**
livre	**free ; vacant ; for hire**
livro *m*	**book**
lixívia *f*	**bleach**
lixo *m*	**rubbish**
loção *f*	**lotion**
loja *f*	**shop**

lombo *m*	**loin** *(cut of meat)*
Londres	**London**
longe	**far**
é longe?	**is it far?**
longo(a)	**long**
lotaria *f*	**lottery**
louça *f*	**dishes ; crockery**
louro(a)	**fair** *(hair)*
louro *m*	**bay leaf** *(herb)*
lua *f*	**moon**
lua-de-mel *f*	**honeymoon**
lugar *m*	**seat** *(theatre)* **; place**
lulas *fpl*	**squid**
luvas *fpl*	**gloves**
luxo *m*	**luxury**
luz *f*	**light**
luzes de presença	**sidelights**
luzes de perigo	**hazard lights**
Lx	*see* **Lisboa**
M.	**underground** *(metro)*
má	*see* **mau**
maçã *f*	**apple**
maçaroca *f*	**corn on the cob**
macho *m*	**male** *(animal)*
macio(a)	**soft ; smooth**
maço *m*	**packet** *(of cigarettes)*
madeira *f*	**wood**
Madeira *f*	**island renowned for its fortified wines**
madrugada *f*	**early morning**
maduro(a)	**ripe**
mãe *f*	**mother**

magro(a)	**thin**
Maio *m*	**May**
maior	**larger**
a maior parte de	**the majority of**
mais	**more**
o/a mais	**the most**
mal	**wrong ; evil**
mala *f*	**suitcase ; bag ; trunk**
malagueta *f*	**chilli**
mal-entendido *m*	**misunderstanding**
mal-estar *m*	**discomfort**
mancha *f*	**stain**
mandar	**to send ; to order**
maneira *f*	**way** *(method)*
manga *f*	**sleeve**
manhã *f*	**morning**
manteiga *f*	**butter**
manter	**to keep ; to maintain**
mão *f*	**hand**
mapa *m*	**map**
mapa das estradas	**road map**
mapa das ruas	**street plan**
máquina *f*	**machine**
máquina fotográfica	**camera**
mar *m*	**sea**
maracujá *m*	**passion fruit**
marca *f*	**brand ; mark**
marcação *f*	**booking ; dialling**
marcar	**to dial** *(phone)* **; to mark**
marcha-atrás *f*	**reverse** *(gear)*
Março *m*	**March**
marco do correio *m*	**pillar box**
maré *f*	**tide**
maré-baixa *f*	**low tide**

maré-cheia *f*	**high tide**
marfim *m*	**ivory**
marido *m*	**husband**
marisco *m*	**seafood ; shellfish**
marmelada *f*	**quince cheese**
marmelo *m*	**quince**
mármore *m*	**marble** *(substance)*
Marrocos	**Morocco**
marroquinaria *f*	**leather goods**
mas	**but**
massa *f*	**dough**
massas	**pasta**
massa folhada	**puff pastry**
matrícula *f*	**number plate**
mau (má)	**bad ; evil**
máximo(a)	**maximum**
mazagrã *m*	**iced coffee and lemon**
me	**me**
mecânico *m*	**mechanic**
média *f*	**average**
medicamento *m*	**medicine**
médico(a) *m/f*	**doctor**
medida *f*	**measure ; size**
médio(a)	**medium**
medusa *f*	**jellyfish**
meia *f*	**stocking ; half**
meia-hora *f*	**half-hour**
meia-noite *f*	**midnight**
meio *m*	**middle**
no meio de	**in the middle of**
meio(a)	**half**
meia garrafa	**a half bottle**
meia de leite	**cup of milky coffee**
meia pensão	**half board**

meio-dia *m* — **midday ; noon**
meio-seco — **medium sweet** *(wine)*
mel *m* — **honey**
melancia *f* — **watermelon**
melão *m* — **melon**
melhor — **best ; better**
meloa *f* — **small round melon**
menina *f* — **Miss ; girl**
menino *m* — **boy**
menor — **smaller ; minor** *(underage)*
menos — **least ; less**
mensagem *f* — **message**
mensal — **monthly**
menstruação *f* — **period** *(menstruation)*
mercado *m* — **market**
mercearia *f* — **grocer's**
merengue *m* — **meringue**
mês *m* — **month**
mesa *f* — **table**
mesmo(a) — **same**
mesquita *f* — **mosque**
metade *f* — **half**
  metade do preço — **half price**
meter — **to put in**
metro *m* — **metre ; underground** *(rail)*
metropolitano *m* — **tube** *(underground)*
meu (minha) — **my ; mine**
mexer — **to move**
  não mexer — **do not touch**
mexilhão *m* — **mussel**
migas à alentejana — **thick bread soup**
mil — **thousand**
milhão *m* — **million**

milho *m*	**maize ; corn**
mim	**me**
minha	*see* **meu**
mínimo(a)	**minimum**
minúsculo(a)	**tiny**
mobília *f*	**furniture**
mochila *f*	**backpack ; rucksack**
moda *f*	**fashion**
moeda *f*	**coin ; currency**
moído(a)	**ground** *(coffee, etc)*
moinho *m*	**windmill**
moinho de café	**coffee grinder**
mola *f*	**peg ; spring** *(coiled metal)*
molhado(a)	**wet**
molho *m*	**sauce ; gravy**
momento *m*	**moment**
montanha *f*	**mountain**
montante *m*	**amount** *(total)*
montra *f*	**shop window**
morada *f*	**address**
moradia *f*	**villa**
morango *m*	**strawberry**
morar	**to live ; to reside**
morcela *f*	**black pudding**
mordedura de insecto *f*	**insect bite**
morder	**to bite**
moreno(a)	**tanned ; dark skinned**
morrer	**to die**
mortadela *f*	**cold meat**
mosaicos *mpl*	**mosaic tiles**
mosca *f*	**fly** *(insect)*
mostarda *f*	**mustard**
mosteiro *m*	**monastery**

mostrador *m*	**dial ; glass counter**
mostrar	**to show**
motocicleta *f*	**motorbike**
motor *m*	**engine ; motor**
motor de arranque	**starter motor**
motorista *m*	**driver**
motorizada *f*	**motorbike**
muçulmano(a)	**Muslim**
mudar	**to change**
mudar-se	**to move house**
muito	**very ; much ; quite** *(rather)*
muitos(as)	**a lot (of) ; many ; plenty (of)**
mulher *f*	**female ; woman ; wife**
multa *f*	**fine**
multidão *f*	**crowd**
mundial	**worldwide**
mundo *m*	**world**
muralhas *fpl*	**ramparts**
muro *m*	**wall**
museu *m*	**museum**
música *f*	**music**

nabo *m*	**turnip**
nacional	**national**
nacionalidade *f*	**nationality ; citizenship**
nada	**nothing**
nada a declarar	**nothing to declare**
nadar	**to swim**
namorada *f*	**girlfriend**
namorado *m*	**boyfriend**
não	**no ; not**
nariz *m*	**nose**
nascer	**to be born**

nascimento *m*	**birth**
nata *f*	**cream**
natação *f*	**swimming**
Natal *m*	**Christmas**
naturalidade *f*	**place of birth**
natureza *f*	**nature**
navio *m*	**ship**
neblina *f*	**mist**
negar	**to refuse**
negativo(a)	**negative**
negócios *mpl*	**business**
negro(a)	**black**
nem: nem ... nem ...	**neither ... nor ...**
nenhum(a)	**none**
neta *f*	**granddaughter**
neto *m*	**grandson**
neve *f*	**snow**
nevoeiro *m*	**fog**
ninguém	**nobody**
nível *m*	**level**
nó *m*	**knot**
nó rodoviário	**motorway interchange**
No.	*see* **número**
nocivo(a)	**harmful**
nódoa *f*	**stain**
noite *f*	**evening ; night**
à noite	**in the evening**
boa noite	**good evening/night**
noivo(a)	**engaged to be married**
nome *m*	**name**
nome próprio	**first name**
nora *f*	**daughter-in-law**
nordeste *m*	**north east**
normalmente	**usually**

noroeste *m* — **north west**
norte *m* — **north**
nós — **we ; us**
nosso(a) — **our**
nota *f* — **note ; banknote**
notar — **to notice**
notícia *f* — **piece of news**
Nova Zelândia *f* — **New Zealand**
Novembro *m* — **November**
novo(a) — **new ; young ; recent**
noz *f* — **nut ; walnut**
noz-moscada *f* — **nutmeg**
nu(a) — **naked**
nublado(a) — **dull** *(weather)* **; cloudy**
número (No.) *m* — **number ; size** *(of clothes, shoes)*
nunca — **never**
nuvem *f* — **cloud**

o — **the** *(masculine)*
objecto *m* — **object**
  objectos perdidos — **lost property ; lost and found**
obra-prima *f* — **masterpiece**
obras *fpl* — **roadworks ; repairs**
obrigado(a) — **thank you**
oceano *m* — **ocean**
ocidental — **western**
oculista *m* — **optician**
óculos *mpl* — **glasses**
  óculos de sol — **sunglasses**
ocupado(a) — **busy ; engaged** *(phone, toilet)*
oeste *m* — **west**
oferecer — **to offer ; to give something**

oferta *f*	**offer ; gift**
olá	**hello**
olaria *f*	**pottery**
óleo *m*	**oil**
óleo dos travões	**brake fluid**
oleoso(a)	**greasy ; oily**
olhar para/por	**to look at/after**
olho *m*	**eye**
onda *f*	**wave** *(on sea)*
onde	**where**
ontem	**yesterday**
óptimo(a)	**excellent**
ora	**now ; well now**
orçamento *m*	**budget**
ordem *f*	**order**
ordenado *m*	**wage**
orelha *f*	**ear**
organizado(a)	**organized**
orquídea *f*	**orchid**
osso *m*	**bone**
ostra *f*	**oyster**
ou	**or**
ourivesaria e joalharia	**goldsmith's and jeweller's**
ouro *m*	**gold**
de ouro	**gold** *(made of gold)*
outono *m*	**autumn**
outro(a)	**other**
outra vez	**again**
Outubro *m*	**October**
ouvido *m*	**ear**
ouvir	**to hear ; to listen (to)**
ovelha *f*	**sheep**
ovo *m*	**egg**
oxigénio *m*	**oxygen**

padaria *f* — **baker's**
pagamento *m* — **payment**
  pagamento a pronto — **cash payment**
pagar — **to pay**
página *f* — **page**
  páginas amarelas — **Yellow Pages**
pago(a) — **paid**
pai *m* — **father**
  pais — **parents**
país *m* — **country**
palácio *m* — **palace**
palavra *f* — **word**
pálido(a) — **pale**
palito *m* — **toothpick**
panado(a) — **fried in egg and breadcrumbs**
pane *f* — **breakdown** *(car)*
panela *f* — **pan ; pot**
pano *m* — **cloth**
pão *m* — **bread ; loaf**
  pão de centeio — **rye bread**
  pão integral — **wholemeal bread**
  pão de ló — **sponge cake**
  pão de milho — **maize bread**
  pão torrado — **toasted bread**
  pão de trigo — **wheat bread**
papel *m* — **paper**
  papel de carta — **writing paper**
  papel de embrulho — **wrapping paper**
  papel higiénico — **toilet paper**
papelaria *f* — **stationer's**
papo-seco *m* — **roll** *(of bread)*
par *m* — **pair ; couple**
para — **for ; towards ; to**
parabéns *mpl* — **congratulations; happy birthday**

pára-brisas *f*	**windscreen**
pára-choques *m*	**bumper**
parafuso *m*	**screw**
paragem *f*	**stop** *(for bus, etc)*
parar	**to stop**
pare	**stop** *(sign)*
pare ao sinal vermelho	**stop when lights are red**
parede *f*	**wall**
parente *m*	**relation** *(family)*
pargo *m*	**sea bream**
parque *m*	**park**
parquímetro *m*	**parking meter**
parte *f*	**part**
parte de frente	**front**
parte de trás	**back**
particular	**private**
partida *f*	**departure**
partidas	**departures**
partir	**to break ; to leave**
a partir de ...	**from ...**
Páscoa *f*	**Easter**
passa *f*	**raisin**
passadeira *f*	**zebra crossing**
passado *m*	**the past**
passado(a): mal passado	**rare** *(steak)*
bem passado	**well done** *(steak)*
passageiro *m*	**passenger**
passagem *f*	**fare ; crossing**
passagem de nível	**level-crossing**
passagem de peões	**pedestrian crossing**
passagem proibida	**no right of way**
passagem subterrânea	**underpass**
passaporte *m*	**passport**
passar	**to pass ; to go by**
pássaro *m*	**bird**

passatempos *mpl* — **entertainment ; hobbies**
passe *m* — **season ticket**
passe — **go** *(when crossing road)* **; walk**
passear — **to go for a walk**
passeio *m* — **walk ; pavement**
pasta *f* — **paste**
  pasta dentífrica — **toothpaste**
pastéis *mpl* — **pastries**
pastel *m* — **pie ; pastry** *(cake)*
  pastel folhado — **puff pastry**
pastelaria *f* — **pastries ; café ; cake shop**
pastilha *f* — **pastille**
  pastilha elástica — **chewing gum**
  pastilhas para a garganta — **throat lozenges**
pataniscas *fpl* — **salted cod fritters**
patinagem *f* — **skating** *(ice)* **; roller-skating**
patinar — **to skate**
pátio *m* — **courtyard**
pato *m* — **duck**
pau *m* — **stick**
pé *m* — **foot**
  a pé — **on foot**
peão *m* — **pedestrian**
peça *f* — **part ; play**
  peças e acessórios — **spares and accessories**
peça... — **ask for...**
pediatra *m/f* — **paediatrician**
pedir — **to ask**
  pedir alguma coisa — **to ask for something**
  pedir emprestado — **to borrow**
peito *m* — **breast ; chest**
peixaria *f* — **fishmonger's**
peixe *m* — **fish**
  peixe congelado — **frozen fish**
peixe-espada *m* — **scabbard fish**

pele *f*	**fur ; skin**
película *f*	**film** *(for camera)*
pensão *m*	**guesthouse**
pensão completa	**full board**
pensão residencial	**boarding house**
meia pensão	**half board**
pensar	**to think**
penso *m*	**sticking plaster**
penso higiénico	**sanitary towel**
pente *m*	**comb**
peões *mpl*	**pedestrians**
pepino *m*	**cucumber**
pepino de conserva	**gherkin**
pequeno(a)	**little ; small**
pequeno-almoço	**breakfast**
pera *f*	**pear**
pera abacate	**avocado pear**
percebes *mpl*	**edible barnacles**
percurso *m*	**route**
perdão	**I beg your pardon ; I'm sorry**
perder	**to lose ; to miss** *(train, etc)*
perdido(a)	**lost**
perdidos e achados	**lost and found ; lost property**
perdiz *f*	**partridge**
pergunta *f*	**question**
fazer uma pergunta	**to ask a question**
perigo *m*	**danger**
perigo de incêndio	**fire hazard**
perigoso(a)	**dangerous**
permitir	**to allow**
perna *f*	**leg**
pérola *f*	**pearl**
pertencer	**to belong**
perto de	**near**
perú *m*	**turkey**

pesado(a)	**heavy**
pêsames *mpl*	**condolences**
pesar	**to weigh**
pesca *f*	**fishing**
pescada *f*	**hake**
pescadinhas *fpl*	**whiting**
pescar	**to fish**
peso *m*	**weight**
pêssego *m*	**peach**
pessoa *f*	**person**
pessoal *adj*	**personal**
pessoal *n*	**staff** *(office, factory)* **; personnel**
petiscos *mpl*	**snacks ; titbits**
petróleo *m*	**oil**
peugas *fpl*	**socks**
picada *f*	**sting**
picado(a)	**stung**
picante	**spicy**
pilha *f*	**pile ; battery** *(for torch)*
pílula *f*	**the pill**
pimenta *f*	**pepper**
pimento *m*	**pepper** *(vegetable)*
pintar	**to paint**
pintura *f*	**painting**
pior	**worse**
piripiri *m*	**hot chilli dressing**
pisca-pisca *m*	**indicator** *(on car)*
piscina *f*	**swimming pool**
piscina aberta	**outdoor swimming pool**
piscina para crianças	**paddling pool**
piso *m*	**floor ; level ; surface**
piso escorregadio	**slippery surface**
pista *f*	**track ; runway**
planta *f*	**plant ; map**

plataforma *f*	**platform**
plateia *f*	**stalls** *(in theatre)*
platinados *fpl*	**points** *(in car)*
pneu *m*	**tyre**
a pressão dos pneus	**tyre pressure**
pó *m*	**dust ; powder**
pó de talco	**talcum powder**
poço *m*	**well**
poder	**to be able**
polegar *m*	**thumb**
polícia *f*	**police** *(force)*
polícia *m*	**policeman ; police officer**
mulher-polícia *f*	**policewoman**
poluição *f*	**pollution**
polvo *m*	**octopus**
pomada *f*	**ointment**
pomada para o calçado	**shoe polish**
pomar *m*	**orchard**
pombo *m*	**pigeon**
ponte *f*	**bridge**
população *f*	**population**
por	**by** *(through)*
por aqui/por ali	**this/that way**
por hora	**per hour**
por pessoa	**per person**
pôr	**to put**
porção *f*	**portion**
porco *m*	**pig ; pork**
por favor	**please**
pormenores *mpl*	**details**
porque	**because**
porquê	**why**
porta *f*	**door**
a porta No. ...	**gate number ...**
porta-bagagens *m*	**boot** *(of car)* **; luggage rack**

porta-chaves *m*	**key ring**
portagem *f*	**toll** *(motorway)*
porta-moedas *m*	**purse**
porteiro *m*	**porter**
porto *m*	**harbour**
Porto : o Porto	**Oporto**
o vinho do Porto	**Port wine**
português (portuguesa)	**Portuguese**
posologia *f*	**dose** *(medicine)*
postal *m*	**postcard**
posto *m*	**post ; job**
posto clínico	**first aid post**
posto de socorros	**first aid centre**
pouco(a)	**little**
pousada *f*	**state-run hotel ; inn**
povo *m*	**people**
povoação *f*	**small village**
praça *f*	**square** *(in town)* ; **market**
praça de táxis	**taxi rank**
praça de touros	**bullring**
praia *f*	**beach ; seaside**
prata *f*	**silver**
prateleira *f*	**shelf**
praticar	**to practise**
prato *m*	**dish ; plate ; course** *(of meal)*
prato da casa	**speciality of the house**
prato do dia	**today's special**
prazer *m*	**pleasure**
prazer em conhecê-lo	**pleased to meet you**
precipício *m*	**cliff ; precipice**
precisar	**to need**
é preciso	**it is necessary**
preço *m*	**price**
preços de ocasião	**bargain prices**
preços reduzidos	**reduced prices**

preencher	**to fill in**
preferir	**to prefer**
prejuízo *m*	**damage**
prémio *m*	**prize**
prenda *f*	**gift**
preocupado(a)	**worried**
preparado(a)	**ready**
presente *m*	**gift ; present**
pressão *f*	**pressure**
pressão dos pneus	**tyre pressure**
presunto *m*	**cured ham**
preto(a)	**black**
primavera *f*	**spring** *(season)*
primeiro(a)	**first**
primeiro andar	**first floor**
primeira classe	**first class** *(seat etc)*
primo(a) *m/f*	**cousin**
princípio *m*	**beginning**
prioridade *f*	**priority**
prioridade à direita	**give way to the right**
prisão *f*	**prison**
ter prisão de ventre	**to be constipated**
privado(a)	**private**
procurar	**to look for**
produto *m*	**product ; proceeds**
produtos alimentares	**foodstuffs**
professor(a) *m/f*	**teacher**
profissão *f*	**profession**
profissão, idade, nome	**profession, age and name**
profundidade *f*	**depth**
profundo(a)	**deep**
proibido(a)	**forbidden**
proibida a entrada	**no entry**
proibido estacionar	**no parking**
proibido fumar	**no smoking**

proibida a paragem	**no stopping**
proibida a passagem	**no access**
proibido pisar a relva	**do not walk on the grass**
proibido tomar banho	**no bathing**
promoção *f*	**special offer ; promotion**
pronto(a)	**ready**
propriedade *f*	**estate** *(property)*
proprietário(a) *m/f*	**owner**
prospecto *m*	**pamphlet**
prótese dentária *f*	**dental fittings**
provar	**to taste ; to try on**
provisório(a)	**temporary**
próximo(a)	**near ; next**
público *m*	**audience ; public**
pudim *m*	**pudding**
pulmão *m*	**lung**
pulseira *f*	**bracelet ; wrist strap**
pulso *m*	**wrist**
pura lã *f*	**pure wool**
purificador do ar *m*	**air freshener**
puxar	**to pull**
puxe	**pull** *(on door)*
quadro *m*	**picture ; painting**
qual	**which**
qualidade *f*	**quality**
quando	**when**
quantidade *f*	**quantity**
quanto	**how much**
quantos(as)?	**how many?**
quanto tempo?	**how long?** *(time)*
quarta-feira *f*	**Wednesday**
quarto *m*	**room ; bedroom**

quarto de banho	**bathroom**
quarto com duas camas	**twin-bedded room**
quarto de casal	**double room**
quarto para uma pessoa	**single room**
quarto	**fourth ; quarter**
• **um quarto de hora**	**a quarter of an hour**
que	**what**
o que é?	**what is it?**
quebra-mar *m*	**pier**
quebrar	**to break**
queda *f*	**fall**
queijada *f*	**cheesecake**
queijo *m*	**cheese**
queimadura *f*	**burn**
queimadura do sol	**sunburn** *(painful)*
queixa *f*	**complaint**
quem	**who**
quente	**hot ; warm**
querer	**to want ; to wish**
quilo(grama) (kg.) *m*	**kilo**
quilómetro *m*	**kilometre**
quinta *f*	**farm**
quinta-feira *f*	**Thursday**
quiosque *m*	**kiosk ; newsstand**
quotidiano(a)	**daily**
R.	see **rua**
rã *f*	**frog**
rabanete *m*	**radish**
rádio *m*	**radio**
radiografia *f*	**X-ray**
raia *f*	**skate** *(fish)*
raiva *f*	**rabies**

raíz *f*	**root**
rapariga *f*	**girl**
rapaz *m*	**boy**
rápido *m*	**express** *(train)*
rápido(a)	**fast**
raposa *f*	**fox**
raqueta *f*	**racket**
rasgar	**to tear**
ratazana *f*	**rat**
rato *m*	**mouse**
R/C	*see* **rés-do-chão**
real	**real ; royal**
reboques *mpl*	**breakdown service**
rebuçado *m*	**sweet** *(confectionery)*
recado *m*	**message**
dar um recado	**to give a message**
receber	**to receive**
receita *f*	**recipe**
receita médica	**prescription**
recepção *f*	**desk** *(in hotel, etc)* **; reception**
recibo *m*	**receipt**
reclamação *f*	**protest ; complaint**
fazer uma reclamação	**to make a complaint**
recolher	**to collect**
recolha de bagagem	**baggage reclaim**
recomendar	**to recommend**
recompensa *f*	**reward**
reconhecer	**to recognize**
recordação *f*	**souvenir**
recordar-se	**to remember**
rede *f*	**net**
redução *f*	**reduction ; discount**
reembolsar	**to reimburse**
refeição *f*	**meal**

refeição da casa	**set menu**
reformado(a) *m/f*	**senior citizen ; retired**
região *f*	**area** *(region)*
região demarcada	**official wine-producing region**
registar	**to register**
regulamentos *mpl*	**regulations**
Reino Unido *m*	**United Kingdom**
relógio *m*	**watch ; clock**
relva *f*	**grass**
não pisar a relva	**keep off the grass**
remédio *m*	**medicine ; remedy**
remetente *m*	**sender**
renda *f*	**lace ; rent**
rendas de bilros	**handwoven lacework**
reparação *f*	**repair**
reparar	**to fix ; to repair**
repartição *f*	**state department**
repetir	**to repeat**
rés-do-chão (R/C) *m*	**ground floor**
reservar	**to reserve**
reserva de lugar	**seat reservation**
reservado(a)	**reserved**
reservar	**to book ; to reserve**
residência *f*	**boarding house ; residence**
residir	**to live**
respirar	**to breathe**
responder	**to answer ; to reply**
resposta *f*	**answer**
restaurante *m*	**restaurant**
retalho *m*	**oddment**
retrosaria *f*	**haberdashery**
reunião *f*	**meeting**
revelar	**to develop** *(photos)* **; to reveal**
revisor *m*	**ticket collector**

revista *f*	**magazine**
ribeiro *m*	**stream**
rins *mpl*	**kidneys**
rio *m*	**river**
rissol *m*	**rissole**
rochas *fpl*	**rocks**
roda *f*	**wheel**
rodovia *f*	**highway**
rolha *f*	**cork**
rolo *m*	**cartridge** *(for camera)* **; roll**
rosto *m*	**face**
roteiro *m*	**guidebook**
roubar	**to steal ; to rob**
roupa *f*	**clothes**
roupa interior	**underwear**
roxo(a)	**purple**
rua (R.) *f*	**street**
rubéola *f*	**German measles**
ruído *m*	**noise**
ruptura *f*	**break**
S.	*see* **São**
sábado *m*	**Saturday**
sabão *m*	**soap**
sabão em flocos	**soapflakes**
sabão em pó	**soap powder**
saber	**to know** *(fact)*
sabonete *m*	**toilet soap**
sabor *m*	**flavour ; taste**
saca-rolhas *m*	**corkscrew**
saco *m*	**bag ; handbag**
saco cama	**sleeping bag**

saco do lixo	**bin bag**
safio *m*	**sea eel**
saia *f*	**skirt**
saída *f*	**exit ; way out**
saídas	**departures**
sair	**to go out ; to come out**
sal *m*	**salt**
sala *f*	**room**
sala de chá	**tea room ; café**
sala de embarque	**lounge** *(at airport)*
sala de espera	**waiting room**
sala de estar	**living room ; lounge**
sala de jantar	**dining room**
salada *f*	**salad**
salão *m*	**hall** *(for concerts, etc)*
salário *m*	**wage ; salary**
saldo *m*	**sale** *(of bargains)*
salgado(a)	**salty**
salmão *m*	**salmon**
salmão fumado	**smoked salmon**
salmonete *m*	**red mullet**
salpicão *m*	**spicy sausage**
salsa *f*	**parsley**
salsicha *f*	**sausage**
salsicharia *f*	**delicatessen**
salteado(a)	**sautéed**
salvar	**to rescue ; to save** *(rescue)*
sandálias *fpl*	**sandals**
sandes *f*	**sandwich**
sandes de fiambre	**ham sandwich**
sanduíche *f*	**sandwich**
sangue *m*	**blood**
sanitários *mpl*	**toilets**
Santo(a) (Sto./Sta.) *m/f*	**saint**
santo(a)	**holy**

santola *f* — **spider crab**
São (S.) *m* — **Saint**
sapataria *f* — **shoe shop**
sapateira *f* — **type of crab**
sapateiro *m* — **shoemaker ; cobbler**
sapato *m* — **shoe**
saquinhos de chá *mpl* — **tea bags**
sarampo *m* — **measles**
sardinha *f* — **sardine**
satisfeito(a) — **happy ; satisfied**
saudação *f* — **greeting**
saudável — **healthy**
saúde *f* — **health**
  saúde! — **cheers!**
se — **if ; whether**
  se faz favor (SFF) — **please**
sé *f* — **cathedral**
secador *m* — **dryer**
secar — **to dry ; to drain** *(tank)*
secção *f* — **department**
seco(a) — **dry**
secretária *f* — **desk**
secretário(a) *m/f* — **secretary**
século *m* — **century**
seda *f* — **silk**
sede *f* — **thirst**
  ter sede — **to be thirsty**
segredo *m* — **secret**
seguinte — **following**
seguir — **to follow**
  seguir pela direita — **keep to your right**
  seguir pela esquerda — **keep to your left**
segunda-feira *f* — **Monday**
segundo *m* — **second** *(time)*

segundo(a) — **second**
- **segundo andar** — **second floor**
- **de segunda classe** — **second class** *(seat, etc)*
- **em segunda mão** — **second-hand**

segurança *f* — **safety**

segurar — **to hold**

seguro *m* — **insurance**
- **seguro contra terceiros** — **third party insurance**
- **seguro contra todos os riscos** — **comprehensive insurance**
- **seguro de viagem** — **travel insurance**

seguro(a) — **safe ; reliable**

seio *m* — **breast**

selecção *f* — **selection**

selo *m* — **stamp**

selvagem — **wild**

sem — **without**

semáforos *mpl* — **traffic lights**

semana *f* — **week**
- **para a semana** — **next week**
- **na semana passada** — **last week**
- **por semana** — **weekly** *(rate, etc)*

semanal — **weekly**

sempre — **always**

senhor *m* — **sir ; gentleman ; you**
- **Senhor** — **Mr**

senhora *f* — **lady ; madam ; you**
- **Senhora** — **Mrs, Ms**
- **senhoras** — **Ladies'**

senhorio(a) *m/f* — **landlord/lady** *(of property)*

sentar-se — **to sit (down)**

sentido *m* — **sense ; meaning**
- **sentido único** — **one-way street**

sentir — **to feel**

ser — **to be**

serviço *m*	**service ; cover charge**
serviço de quartos	**room service**
serviço (não) incluído	**service (not) included**
serviço permanente	**24-hour service**
sessão *f*	**session ; performance**
Setembro *m*	**September**
seu (sua)	**his ; her ; your**
sexta-feira *f*	**Friday**
SFF	*see* **se faz por favor**
shampô *m*	**shampoo**
significar	**to mean**
sim	**yes**
simpático(a)	**nice ; friendly**
sinal *m*	**signal ; deposit** *(part payment)*
sinal de impedido	**engaged tone**
sinal de marcação	**dialling tone**
sinal de trânsito	**road sign**
sino *m*	**bell**
sirva-se fresco	**serve cool** *(on label)*
sítio *m*	**place ; spot**
situado(a)	**situated**
só	**only ; alone**
sobre	**over ; on top of**
sobre o mar	**overlooking the sea**
sobrecarga *f*	**excess load ; surcharge**
sobremesa *f*	**dessert**
sobressalente	**spare**
a roda sobressalente	**spare wheel**
sobretudo *m*	**overcoat** *(man's)*
sócio *m*	**member ; partner**
socorro *m*	**help ; assistance**
socorro 115	**emergency service 999**
socorros e sinistrados	**accidents and emergencies**
sol *m*	**sun**
solteiro(a)	**single** *(not married)*

solúvel	**soluble**
som *m*	**sound**
soma *f*	**amount** *(sum)*
sombra *f*	**shadow** *(in sun)*
sono *m*	**sleep**
sopa *f*	**soup**
sorte *f*	**luck ; fortune**
boa sorte	**good luck**
sorvete *m*	**water-ice ; sorbet**
sótão *m*	**attic**
soutien *m*	**bra**
sua	*see* **seu**
subida *f*	**rise ; ascent**
subir	**to go up**
sudeste *m*	**south east**
sudoeste *m*	**south west**
suficiente	**enough**
sujo(a)	**dirty**
sul *m*	**south**
sumo *m*	**juice**
suor *m*	**sweat**
supermercado *m*	**supermarket**
supositório *m*	**suppository**
surdo(a)	**deaf**
surf *m*	**surfing**
tabacaria *f*	**tobacconist's ; newsagent**
tabaco *m*	**tobacco**
tabela *f*	**list ; table**
taberna *f*	**wine bar**
tabuleiro *m*	**tray**
taça *f*	**cup**

tacão *m*	**heel**
talão *m*	**voucher**
talco *m*	**talc**
talheres *mpl*	**cutlery**
talho *m*	**butcher's**
talvez	**perhaps**
tamanho *m*	**size**
também	**also ; too**
tamboril *m*	**monkfish**
tampa *f*	**lid ; cover ; top ; cap**
tampões *mpl*	**tampons**
tanto(a)	**so much**
tão	**so**
tapete *m*	**carpet ; rug**
tapetes e carpetes	**rugs and carpets**
tarde *f*	**afternoon**
boa tarde	**good afternoon**
tarde	**late** *(in the day)*
tarifa *f*	**charge ; rate**
tarifas de portagem	**toll charges**
tarte *f*	**tart**
tarte de amêndoa	**almond tart**
tasca *f*	**tavern ; wine bar ; restaurant**
taxa *f*	**fee**
taxa de juro	**interest rate**
taxa normal	**peak-time rate**
taxa reduzida	**off-peak rate**
teatro *m*	**theatre**
tecido *m*	**fabric ; tissue ; cloth**
tejadilho *m*	**roof rack**
telecomandado(a)	**remote-controlled**
teleférico *m*	**cable car**
telefone *m*	**telephone**
telefonista *f*	**operator**

televisão *f*	**television**
televisor *m*	**television set**
telhado *m*	**roof**
temperatura *f*	**temperature**
tempero *m*	**dressing** *(for salad)* **; seasoning**
tempestade *f*	**storm**
tempo *m*	**weather ; time** *(duration)*
tempo inteiro	**full-time**
tempo parcial	**part-time**
temporada *f*	**season**
temporário(a)	**temporary**
tenda *f*	**tent**
ténis *m*	**tennis**
tenro(a)	**tender** *(meat)*
tensão *f*	**tension**
tensão arterial alta/baixa	**high/low blood pressure**
tentar	**to try**
ter	**to have**
ter febre	**to have a temperature**
terça-feira *f*	**Tuesday**
terceiro(a)	**third**
terceiro andar	**third floor**
para a terceira idade	**for the elderly**
termas *fpl*	**spa**
termo *m*	**(vacuum) flask**
termómetro *m*	**thermometer**
terra *f*	**earth ; ground**
terraço *m*	**veranda ; balcony**
terramoto *m*	**earthquake**
terreno *m*	**ground ; land**
tesoura *f*	**scissors**
tesouro *m*	**treasure**
testemunha *f*	**witness**
tímido(a)	**shy**

tingir	**to dye**
tinta *f*	**ink ; paint**
tinturaria *f*	**dry-cleaner's**
tio(a) *m/f*	**uncle/aunt**
tipo *m*	**sort ; kind**
tira-nódoas *m*	**stain remover**
tirar	**to remove ; to take out** *(tooth)*
tiro *m*	**shot**
toalha *f*	**towel**
toalhete de rosto *m*	**face cloth ; flannel** *(for washing)*
toalhetes refrescantes *mpl*	**baby wipes**
tocar	**to touch ; to ring ; to play**
tocar piano	**to play the piano**
todo(a)	**all ; the whole**
toda a gente	**everyone**
todas as coisas	**everything**
em toda a parte	**everywhere**
toldo *f*	**sunshade** *(on beach)*
tomada *f*	**socket ; power point**
tomar	**to take**
tomar banho	**to bathe ; to take a bath**
tomar antes de se deitar	**take before going to bed**
tomar em jejum	**take on an empty stomach**
tomar ... vezes ao dia	**take ... times a day**
tomate *m*	**tomato**
tonelada *f*	**ton**
toranja *f*	**grapefruit**
torcer	**to twist ; to turn**
torneio *m*	**tournament**
torneira *f*	**tap**
tornozelo *m*	**ankle**
torrada *f*	**toast**
torre *f*	**tower**
torto(a)	**twisted**
tosse *f*	**cough**

tosta *f*	**toasted sandwich**
tosta de queijo	**toasted cheese sandwich**
tostões: 25 tostões	**= 2.5 escudos**
totobola *m*	**football pools**
totoloto *m*	**lottery**
toucinho *m*	**bacon**
tourada *f*	**bullfight**
touro *m*	**bull**
tóxico(a)	**poisonous ; toxic**
trabalhar	**to work** *(person)*
trabalho *m*	**work**
trabalhos na estrada	**roadworks**
tradução *f*	**translation**
traduzir	**to translate**
tráfego *m*	**traffic**
tranquilo(a)	**calm ; quiet**
transferir	**to transfer**
trânsito *m*	**traffic**
trânsito condicionado	**restricted traffic**
trânsito proibido	**no entry**
transpiração *f*	**perspiration ; sweat**
transportar	**to transport ; to carry**
transtorno *m*	**upset ; inconvenience**
trás: para trás	**backwards**
no banco de trás	**in the back** *(of car)*
a parte de trás	**back**
tratamento *m*	**treatment**
tratar de	**to treat ; to deal with**
travar	**to brake**
travessa *f*	**lane** *(in town)* **; serving dish**
travessia *f*	**crossing** *(voyage)*
travões *mpl*	**brakes**
trazer	**to bring ; to carry**
triângulo *m*	**warning triangle**

tribunal *m*	**court**
trigo *m*	**wheat**
triste	**sad**
trocar	**to exchange ; to change**
troco *m*	**change** *(money)*
trocos	**small change**
trovoada *f*	**thunderstorm**
truta *f*	**trout**
tu	**you** *(informal)*
tubo *m* *(car)*	**exhaust pipe ; tube ; hose**
tudo	**everything ; all**
turista *m/f*	**tourist**
ultimamente	**lately ; recently**
último(a)	**last ; latest**
ultrapassar	**to overtake ; to pass**
um(a)	**a ; an ; one**
unha *f*	**nail** *(on finger, toe)*
único(a)	**single** *(not double)* **; unique**
unidade *f*	**unit** *(hi-fi, etc)* **; unity**
unir	**to join**
universidade *f*	**university ; college**
urgência *f*	**urgency**
urtiga *f*	**nettle**
usado(a)	**used** *(car, etc)*
usar	**to use ; to wear**
uso *m*	**use**
uso externo	**for external use**
útil	**useful**
utilização *f*	**use**
utilizar	**to use**
uva *f*	**grape**

vaca *f*	**cow**
vacina *f*	**vaccination**
vagão *m*	**railway carriage ; coach**
vagão-restaurante *m*	**buffet car**
vagar	**to be vacant**
vago(a)	**vague ; vacant**
vale *m*	**valley**
valer	**to be worth**
validação de bilhetes	**punch ticket here** *(on bus, etc)*
válido(a)	**valid**
válido até...	**valid until...**
valor *m*	**value**
válvula *f*	**valve ; tap**
vapor *m*	**steam**
varanda *f*	**veranda ; balcony**
variado(a)	**varied**
varicela *f*	**chickenpox**
vários(as)	**several**
vazio(a)	**empty**
vegetal *m*	**vegetable**
vegetais congelados	**frozen vegetables**
vegetariano(a)	**vegetarian**
veículo *m*	**vehicle**
veículos pesados	**heavy goods vehicles**
vela *f*	**sail ; sailing**
vela *f*	**spark plug ; candle**
velho(a)	**old**
velocidade *f*	**gear ; speed**
velocidade limitada	**speed limit in force**
velocímetro *m*	**speedometer**
vencimento *m*	**wage ; salary**
venda *f*	**sale** *(in general)*
venda proibida	**not for public sale**
vendas e reparações	**sales and repairs**

vender	**to sell**
vende-se	**for sale**
veneno *m*	**poison**
vento *m*	**wind**
ventoinha *f*	**fan** *(electric)*
ver	**to see ; to look at**
verão *m*	**summer**
verdade *f*	**truth**
não é verdade?	**isn't it?**
verdadeiro(a)	**true**
verde	**green**
vergas *fpl*	**wicker goods**
verificar	**to check**
vermelho(a)	**red**
verniz *m*	**varnish**
vertigem *f*	**dizziness ; vertigo**
vespa *f*	**wasp**
véspera *f*	**the day before ; the eve**
vestiário *m*	**cloakroom ; changing room**
vestido *m*	**dress**
vestir	**to dress ; to wear**
vestir-se	**to get dressed**
vestuário *m*	**clothes**
veterinário(a) *m/f*	**vet**
vez *f*	**time**
às vezes	**occasionally ; sometimes**
uma vez	**once**
duas vezes	**twice**
muitas vezes	**often**
via *f*	**lane**
via	**via**
via aérea	**by air mail**
via nasal	**to be inhaled**
via oral	**orally**
viaduto *m*	**viaduct ; flyover**

viagem *f*	**trip ; journey**
viagem de negócios	**business trip**
viajante *m/f*	**traveller**
viajar	**to travel**
vida *f*	**life**
vidros *mpl*	**glassware**
vila *f*	**small town**
vinagre *m*	**vinegar**
vindima *f*	**harvest** *(of grapes)*
vinho *m*	**wine**
vir	**to come**
virar	**to turn**
vire à direita	**turn right**
vire à esquerda	**turn left**
vírgula *f*	**comma**
visitar	**to visit**
vista *f*	**view**
com linda vista	**with a beautiful view**
visto *m*	**visa**
vitela *f*	**veal**
viúvo(a) *m/f*	**widower/widow**
vivenda *f*	**chalet ; villa**
viver	**to live**
vivo(a)	**alive**
vizinho(a) *m/f*	**neighbour**
você(s)	**you**
volante *m*	**steering wheel**
volta *f*	**turn**
à volta de	**about**
em volta de	**around**
dar uma volta	**to go for a short walk/ride**
voltagem *f*	**voltage**
voltar	**to return** *(go/come back)*
volto já	**I will be back in a minute**

vomitar	**to vomit**
voo *m*	**flight**
voo fretado	**charter flight**
voo normal	**scheduled flight**
vos	**you ; to you**
vós	**you**
vosso	**yours**
voz *f*	**voice**
vulcão *m*	**volcano**
WC	**toilet**
wind-surf *m*	**windsurfing**
xadrez *m*	**chess**
xarope *m*	**syrup**
xarope para a tosse	**cough linctus**
xerez *m*	**sherry**
zero	**zero ; nought**
zona *f*	**zone**
zona azul	**permitted parking zone**
zona de banhos	**swimming area**
zona interdita	**no thoroughfare**